About the author

Ian Clark moved to London stayed. For twenty six years the Prince Edward Theatre i. experience he describes as "Wonderful". In 2005 he became the Group Bars & Catering Manager for Delfont Mackintosh Theatres Ltd, a rewarding role because of the unusual challenges it gives.

Some people find him aloof and sceptical, especially when he tends not to show emotion; making it difficult for them to know what he is thinking or feeling. He rises to the occasion when dealing with problems, the harder they are, the more determined he is to overcome. This book is witness to that.

Living in Manor Park, in London's East End, he walks daily to the Ilford gym for yoga practice or swimming. The local children amuse him with chalk drawings and games. To them he is someone who knows what is important; - laughing loudly, losing Frisbees in trees, bubbles, dancing in the rain. His biggest disappointment is how adults lose sight of what is important.

With thanks to Erum Masood of Memediaglobal.com

4:26 a.m.

Ian Clark

To Kerry,
Glad you
enjoyed it. Hope
you get more on the
next read.
Ian Clark
14/11/15

New Generation Publishing

Introduction

4:26 a.m. on 25th August 2011 the phone rang. Jane at a desperate moment had called for help. That night, detailed in chapter 3, forced a look at me; it became clear I am different. Events over my life, personal characteristics and physiology have taken on significance. An anomaly exposed by circumstances. This book is the result. There is no revelation of god, or religion. Belief and justification, where possible, have been avoided. It is based on reality, sense and observation. Dates and timings calculated from what could be remembered. The only changes are some names; after all, everyone is entitled to their privacy.

The first four chapters are my story, clues. The following seven look at what it means, answers, well, some of them. Chapter 12, 'The deep end' gazes at group and cultural aspects, including wild speculation. Finally, there is a summary.

The book is for people who struggle with emotions trying to burst forth; Sufferers of night terrors, panic attacks, and hag phenomena (sleep paralysis); Often feeling unable to describe the emotion and turmoil felt inside. Also for the worlds of science and medicine which appear blind to what now seems obvious, saying why it happens, and words fail; how self-imposed ignorance exists in those disciplines.

I have no medical or scientific qualifications, nor proof for these claims. There are contradictions in the book. Some conclusions will be wrong, however, the main points look solid. Many statements are blunt, 'ifs', 'buts' and 'maybes' discarded wherever possible. Beyond this book, there is more to be understood. It exposes ignorance, mine as well as others. Each and every reader will understand, coming to conclusions in their own way, and will be more than capable of adding scepticism and doubt. The understanding of what happened and my apparent difference, could help others. It should push forward our knowledge of people, emotions and the mind. Wonderful to think it will change the world, reality is, more likely to be ignored or denied.

Whatever happens, some mornings will start with the feeling of not being human, and end in the understanding I am; just not sure what everyone else is.

Chapter 1: The early years

In November 1957 Graham became the first born of John and Helen Clark. Three years later, in October, I arrived. Dad's mum, Madge, was there. Her dislike was instant, saying to Mum "He looks just like your father!" Not a compliment. Her attitude set, taking as little interest in me as possible. She was not a bad person, and often roared with laughter at the mischief Graham got up to. When Kim joined the family in 1963, Madge doted on her, having a soft spot for baby girls. There was no space in her world for me.

At six weeks old I was taken to hospital for a smallpox jab. Then such inoculations were common in an attempt to wipe out the disease. Most people found it painful, some of the medical profession claimed such pain was all in the mind. It seems strange they were so dismissive of other people's discomfort. Apparently when the scratch was given, after turning pale, my eyes rolled up and I fainted. The watching nurse said "Well, that's not psychological is it?"

From birth Graham was active and energetic. Smart, grasping things quickly, such as using a knife and fork. Progressing rapidly from cutlery to climbing ropes and getting into the sort of trouble young boys are supposed to. It was a shock for our parents; their second child needed only feeding, somewhere warm to sleep and a clean nappy. By two years old I hadn't spoken; some gabbling, but nothing intelligible. There are people who feel it is true today. Because of not speaking the local council agreed to a place in nursery school. The school consisted of two chalets set back from the main road on a large patch of grass with fencing all the way round and a wooden gate. One of the most exciting events was when 'Tufty' the giant squirrel came to visit on behalf of the road safety campaign. Everyone knew it was a man in costume, but was still exciting for young children.

One day, during the spring of 1964, my grandfather, Bernard, drove me to the nursery school in a works van. Arriving outside the school he leaned over and opened the door for me. Walking up to the gate, speaking may have been a problem, reading wasn't; the sign on the gate said school was closed. The works van disappeared into the distance. Despite jumping up and down, and shouting to get his attention, he did not hear; and did not return. It was wet, cold and lonely by the gate. No one appeared. The cold has always hurt; even mild days were spent with numb fingers and toes. It was too much to bear. After a few minutes the decision to walk home was made. Not knowing the way back, the van's direction was the only choice. Walking down the road, cottages appeared on the right. We had visited one a few months before. Which cottage though? Would they be in? I didn't really know them. Better than risk stopping, the walking continued. Just past the cottages was the railway bridge. Part of the journey in the van always included crossing the bridge. The bridge was crossed, and the town hall came into sight. It was close to the bus station, which was at the end of the road we lived on. At last I knew where I was. It was a relief to know somewhere was warm and soon could be there. Eventually reaching the works yard, walking down the drive, and in through the back door I sat in front of the coal burner. It was nice to thaw, and regain feeling. Mum and Dad were surprised by my appearance, since no one had been to collect me. After questioning and a call to the nursery the following week, they worked out what happened. Madge was furious with Bernard. It is likely he suffered her wrath for quite some time. She may not have liked me, but was protective over grandchildren.

One of my earliest memories is during a summer, probably 1965, chasing Kim, through the kitchen out the backdoor and into the garden, where she hid under the window. It was a beautiful day. Graham, was in the garden, Mum was at the sink. In my mind there is strange shadowy image of the porch surrounding the backdoor. On the kitchen wall are fold-away scales. The porch was not built until years later. The scales were put up in about 1968. My memories have adapted and changed; mixing and merging together. There is no attempt to change them further or worry about it, just accept it as the way things are remembered, no matter how inaccurate.

The not talking was a serious concern for my parents. In 1965 primary school was due to start. Kim was already speaking. In desperation a reel to reel tape recorder was borrowed from a friend of the family, and put in Madge's house, she lived two doors away from us. Graham and I went round one evening to visit, we were shown how to use this wonderful machine with big clunky buttons. Talking began almost immediately. The evening and tape recorder are easy to recall, so much fun. It was disappointing to never use it again. People should always be careful what they wish for, from then on everyone complained I wouldn't shut up; as true today as it was then. Chatterbox, a perfect description.

St Mary's was our primary school; it was not a nice place. Lunchtimes were spent hiding from the two gangs of boys who dominated my year. Mrs Bishop my first teacher, would watch impassively from a window whilst victims were attacked and bullied. There were two gang leaders, who will remain nameless for fear of litigation. One went on to a successful naval career, the other spent considerable time at her majesty's pleasure. It has made me question leadership skills and what they entail. There were bad teachers, and good teachers. I remember with fondness my fourth year teacher Mr Trupp as gentle and encouraging, often showing good humour. Mrs. Palmer, the music teacher was energetic and enthusiastic, no matter how badly you sang she was pleased for everyone to join in. The quality of the school was poor. Mum, horrified to discover at seven years old Graham had not been taught the alphabet, immediately set about teaching him the alphabet song.

I frequently suffered coughs and colds. Madge

3

complained all photographs of me were either coughing, or pulling up trousers with one hand because of my slim hips. One time in the first year of primary school I was off sick, again. Sitting in bed and complaining of being bored, Mum suggested we read a book. She started reading with me and was astounded when passing the book over, I took it and read with ease.

Madge was a strange mixture, kind and generous, yet with a bitter, unpleasant streak. She organised family bingo and thought nothing of supplying prizes. Or suddenly appearing in the works yard, carrying a tray filled with mugs of tea for all the workers. With me she was unable to control the sharp tongue. If visiting her, and the spite flowed I would simply turn round and go straight home. There is little recollection of those events, though the unpleasantness was evident. One time Bernard was driving us through the countryside; "Stick out your tongue" she said. Obliging, the tongue came out. "Yuck! It's all coated. I've never met a child like you". I turned and watched countryside pass the window. There was no conversation to be had. When such things happened I didn't think about it. Looking back my sub-conscious has been kind enough to guide and look after me, turning away from unpleasantness to watch the world pass from a distance.

Graham, Kim and I attended Sunday school. There was storytelling, making music, drawing, crayoning and painting; things every child enjoys. The religious side, however, none of us believed or took to. It bothered me privately. The thought people were forcing belief by exposure was insidious. Aesop's fables were not a problem; they dealt with nice easy, simple stories and made sense. God, a different matter altogether. One time Mum recalls me walking into the kitchen and saying "I don't know if I'm thinking about God; or if that means I believe in him". The problem was thinking about something implies belief; otherwise there is nothing to think about. The issue was resolved when realising the

4

opposite is true; thinking about something implies disbelief; otherwise there is nothing to think about. Surely something to give the most ardent believer pause for thought.

Dad was charismatic, good-looking, intelligent, self-centred and without conscience. Graham and Kim loved him dearly. Graham was the energetic complete boy; even as an adult, men and women admired him, and still do. A friend of the family once described him as a man's man. Kim was pretty and a princess in the world of boys. Both were sociable and blossomed in the presence of others. They needed company, and found it difficult to be alone. Even though the company of others in small groups is enjoyable, I was happiest left to my own devices and would play with Lego for hours on end in my room. Dad did not understand and would at times be nasty to me when it suited him. A particular episode happened when I was six years old. One evening Dad sat at the end of the table, Graham to his right, and Kim to the left, Mum stood by the kitchen sink. Walking into the kitchen there were no sounds. Dinner was already on the table. I sat opposite Dad. Picking up the knife and fork, you could have heard a pin drop. Cutting the meat on my plate. They were all waiting. Raised a piece of meat with the fork, tension hung in the air. Mouth closed around the fork prongs. Dad smashed his knife and fork down, glaring, yelling "Why can't you eat quietly?" He stood up, pushing his full plate away and saying "That's it, I've had enough. I'm going out" To this day I remember silent tears dripping onto the food now tasting of nothing. None of us looked at each other during the rest of the meal. Years later we guessed he had a date and needed an excuse to get out of the house.

Apparently Dad took many years to get used to Mum's cooking of what he referred to as 'raw vegetables'. She had a modern outlook on cooking, using only a minimum of salt. It was not even on the table. A trend I continue today. Friends have commented my occasional cooking attempts could do with more cooking, and definitely more

5

salt.

In some ways we were fortunate as children, there were lots of Xmas presents, mostly from our parents. We would wake up on Xmas day in our rooms surrounded by dozens of gifts. Inevitably one of mine was a ginger cake from my other Grandmother, Marjory. As a child I liked ginger and ate quantities of it in everything. It was an easy gift for her to do, including birthdays.

We were allowed to choose our own wallpaper. Whilst each room was being decorated Graham and I shared rooms. My nonstop talking drove him to despair. One night when we were supposed to be sleeping he called out to Mum, "Mum. Mum, Ian won't shut up. He won't stop talking" Mum peered round the door. Words tumbled out, "I can't help it. It starts in my tummy and it bubbles up, and I just have to let it out". Mum smiled and closed the door.

Dark dreams visited from an early age, what most people would call nightmares. One of falling into a wide deep pit, with hands coming from holes in the walls reaching towards me. Another, being chased by a Minotaur. It was terrifying, running away hopeless, always the same distance behind me. Running harder and faster made no difference, eventually getting to where I couldn't breathe. A grim physically imposing creature, filled with anger though without noise or showing emotion. On waking I often associated it with Graham, but never wondering why.

How things worked and why, fascinated me, whether it was mechanical or electrical. Always trying to make sense of the world. When speech arrived I became in technical terms a 'smartass'. This was annoying for everyone. Equally, glib answers that glossed over facts or reality would annoy me, though I didn't talk to anyone about this. It was a conundrum. Being shy and quiet by nature, but trying to understand and argue back. My parents were exasperated by this as much as by previous silence. Mum often used the phrase "If you, 'Yes But' me one more time…" and more than once Mum and Dad would delight in saying "You're wrong. You're wrong", almost in relief.

One night, when we were back in our own rooms, I was in bed trying to sleep. The sound of a sledge hammer could be heard in the background. Distinct, powerful and steady. It seemed strange men working during the night. This went on for about twenty minutes. Curiosity got the better of me, as soon as I moved though, it stopped. The side of my head had been resting on my hand. It was the pulse against the ear making a pounding noise. Surprising how loud it sounded, and felt.

Sometimes in the morning Mum would walk into my bedroom and open the curtains. Like many people I would wake bleary eyed with a desire to continue sleeping. Sometimes though Graham would try to sneak in. No matter how quiet he was I would be awake and know he was there. Never moving or letting him realise, just carried on pretending to be asleep. Strangely, I was never aware of when my parents came in during Xmas Eve to fill the room with presents.

My teeth didn't get the cleaning or attention they deserved though regular visits to the dentist were made. Our dentist Mr. Gebbles, a pleasant man, would examine teeth, whilst humming and singing to himself. Tunes would alter as decay was found, usually sticking to a note like tuning a piano whilst tapping the particular tooth. He would inject the anaesthetic, and immediately drill out the decay. It was painful, sweat would run from my clenched fists. The rest of the day spent in throbbing numbness. We were with him for several years. On the last visit he sent me out to the waiting room, allowing the anaesthetic to take effect before drilling the tooth. He had either discovered, or been informed how it is supposed to work. The first and only time he did not inflict pain. Our next dentist was Mr. Black. On my first visit he used a new anaesthetic. It felt as though my chest was rising up to the ceiling and about to explode, but without pain, just an amazing sense of exhilaration. The sensation was similar to some of the exciting and frightening dreams. He explained it was based upon adrenaline, designed to make capillaries contract and deprive nerves of blood, thereby stopping the pain signals.

I was a nervous timid child. Mum noticed thumb sucking and told me to stop, explaining it wasn't healthy. To her astonishment it stopped immediately. Previously she thought children needed telling several times before doing as told. She realised I would do things as long as there was a reason. Like other young children, anxiety would give me sweaty hands and a tummy ache. It was difficult to control tears. My eyes would water for the slightest reason. A problem that persists today. Crying is always alone, even in public, but watery eyes are difficult to stop anytime.

I felt like Superman. Not the super powers, but knowing the importance of helping people, understanding his loneliness and being apart from others. Real strength was not physical, it was wrestling the terrible demons inside, and out.

Marjory, often used deception to get her own way, simply because Grandfather was a bully. At times it was like "My Big, Fat Greek Wedding" when the women are letting the father believe it is his idea the daughter work for her aunt. It was Marjory's way of life, telling little white lies. The difficulty was remembering them all. Reality thinned, lies took on a life of their own. Any sense of humour died years ahead of her. She was intelligent, but those deceptions, becoming self-deceptions, cost her dearly.

One evening Graham, Mum and I were in the front room. Graham asked Mum "What causes the tides?" I immediately said "It's the moon". He glared and said "No it's not". A heated discussion began. Eventually leaving them and going upstairs to bed. Years later Mum admitted, he'd said "I know it's the moon, but I hate it when he's right".

We had a battery radio in the kitchen. When the house

was empty the casing would come off to expose a circuit board. If the connections were shorted using a metal spoon it made wonderful sounds. It was possible to put the sounds together to make a tune; my attempts were awful. It would be lovely to say I knew how it worked, but really had no idea of how the noises were made or what was happening.

Swimming lessons in primary school were compulsory. The school spent several years teaching pupils to swim, in my case, without success. The technique used was to stand in the pool two metres away from the edge. Then launch yourself at the side pulling with breast stroke. I would tense up, becoming ever more terrified of water. It was frustrating, others were learning to swim. Graham and Kim could swim long before leaving primary school. In the summer holiday break between moving schools I decided to teach myself, and did so by reasoning it out. In the shallow end I could crouch underwater whilst holding my breath. The next time crouching with open eyes. Now taking a step forward, using my arms to pull through the water. This time, no stepping, just pull with the arms using breast stroke. When secondary school started, swimming half a mile was easy. Also the joy of swimming underwater whilst holding my breath, was out of this world. So wonderful, even today.

Chapter 2: Teenage time

Banbury School was the sixth biggest school in Europe. There were four halls, Stanbridge, Wykham, Broughton and Drayton. Every hall contained four years; those years were split into four classes of thirty pupils each. The Upper school was sandwiched between Stanbridge and Broughton, it held years five, six and seven. It also contained the science block and language lab, which had about ten classrooms each. I was put in Stanbridge, the old grammar school. The English teacher, Mrs. Brookes sat me by the window. Unfortunately my habit of staring out the window and day-dreaming annoyed her. Day-dreaming could not be switched off. Mrs. Brookes reduced it by moving me to the centre of the classroom, but did not stop it entirely. She was an excellent teacher, passionate about her subject, fair, without indulgences of favouritism or bullying. Once commenting about the time it takes for the earth to travel around the sun; it struck me as unlikely the earth takes exactly 365 days and 6 hours to make the journey. I said maybe a leap year was removed every hundred years, or an extra one put in somewhere. She became annoyed and said "Don't talk rubbish, it's why we have leap years" She hadn't listened to what was said. Years later I discovered this is exactly what happens, every hundred years a leap year is removed to keep accuracy.

During secondary school Dad's alcoholism and bad behaviour destroyed his marriage and the business. He bankrupted himself, nothing was left from his excesses and self-indulgences. Mum and Dad divorced.

I was in the cubs, then the scouts for several years. We would go camping in Horley. It was an artificial wood composed of firs, all pruned to grow tall and straight. Camping trips would range from two people to the entire Oxfordshire scouting community. One Easter weekend three of us went camping. The scout master would come and check on us during the day and return home in the evening. Each night over the weekend we saw figures dancing round a large fire in the woods. We sat huddled around our own fire for most of the night, frightened, eventually going into the tents and falling asleep. In the morning when we woke they would be gone. There was no sign of their activity, other than the occasional fragment of charred wood. We told the scout master, he laughed and said it was normal over Easter.

One particular windy season whilst camping, five of us were in the woods. I gave everyone a lecture on awareness, "If you hear a tree falling, don't just run, look and see where it's coming from" We walked on, about 30 seconds later there was a tremendous cracking sound, I ran. Everyone said the tree landed exactly where I had stood. Felt like a twit, a live twit admittedly, but a twit all the same. One of those times when words come back to bite. Ouch! Several times my sub-conscious has stepped in and helped in various situations. It's the smarter of the two of us; and probably has answers to questions I haven't even thought of.

My first year biology teacher was Mrs. Swann who taught by the book. She gave us the definition of life. Apparently there were nine criteria that defined a living thing. She promised if we found anything with all nine criteria she would absolutely agree it was alive. Unfortunately it never occurred to her, or the students including me, if the criteria were applied to a city it would be alive. In fact it would work for any group of animals. It might be argued such a group is a living thing, but is that biology or philosophy?

A.C. Pennington taught chemistry, and was also a reading tutor. A book would be chosen, read, and then discussed during the lesson. One of mine was "Cry the beloved country" by Alan Paton. It is about South Africa and its troubles during the first half of the twentieth century. I said the book was not about racism, but poor communication between people. Mr. Pennington stared at me for a while, then asked "Did you watch television last night?" puzzled I said "No". He continued "If you had told me this last week I would have said you were a liar, and hadn't read the book." "The author was on television last night and that's pretty much what he said". I was not his favourite pupil (not that he had favourites), but from then on he regarded me differently, as someone who could think for themselves.

As with primary school it was difficult to fit into Stanbridge, being seen as clever and different. Despite what we are told, different, makes others uncomfortable. Sometimes teachers would be annoyed by awkward questions, preferring the ones in text books. For me there was a sense of isolation and alienation. Teenage years led to the discovery of new physical attributes. Lunchtimes many of us would play a game of ball-tick. One person would start with a tennis ball. They were 'it' and from a standing position would throw the ball to hit other people. Once hit you joined the throwers team. You couldn't move with the ball, but could throw it to someone else in your team. The game was over when everyone had been hit. I was inevitably the last person left, it was practically unknown for me to be hit, and the game would simply stop. You were allowed to knock the ball away using your knuckles; something I never did only ever dodging it, managing to twist and turn avoiding the ball no matter how hard or quickly it was thrown.

In the middle of the afternoon during an English lesson, Mrs. Brookes was missing along with half the class. The rest of us were sat towards the back of the room, almost everyone was behind me. People were chatting, doing nothing in particular. Whilst staring at the board, I was aware of an object being thrown at me from behind. Knowing where it was, and without thinking my left hand extended out to the side, palm facing back, and thumb pointing down. Turning my head at the same time to see and catch the object. It was a comb. The rest of the class gasped, they saw it done without any apparent way for me

12

to know it had been thrown. The comb flicked out of my hand catching a girl, Claire Michelle, on the head. She was cross, complaining 'no need to do that'. The class returned to chatting.

The quality of teachers varied. Mr Orchard a PE instructor was also my second and fourth year form tutor. Understanding to all pupils, and possessing a good sense of humour. One year he roped several boys into dressing up in tutu's to perform the 'Knockerova' ballet for the school, me included. He quite rightly said it would be fun, nothing to be taken too seriously. Boys who thought themselves leaders bottled out. A clever man who did not make assumptions about others, and one of the few teachers to tackle bullying effectively and immediately, not getting cross, but dealing with the perpetrators there and then.

One chemistry teacher prepared us for the joys of 'A' level chemistry by demonstrating an experiment. He mixed some chemicals together producing a test tube of dark liquid and held it for what seemed like a minute. Suddenly it cleared. He smiled, putting it down, "Well, what happened?" I replied "Did it go through a lot of chemical changes and it so happens the last one is to go clear?" "Not really." he said. No one else spoke. "Does it have to build up and then suddenly change?" Again he replied "Not really." "These are the sort of things you will be dealing with in 'A' level." He started talking about what the syllabus would contain. I smiled, and then said "Does it make its own catalyst?" He stared round the rest of the class avoiding my gaze, "He doesn't give up, does he?", "Yes, it does make its own catalyst".

Mr Postlethwaite, was one of two excellent physics teachers, neither of whom accepted information at face value. He made sure understanding was key to his lessons, and was enamoured of the Greeks and their intellectual approach to physics problems. He once described how, in ancient times, a man looked down a well and could see the sun's reflection below. Meanwhile a few hundred miles away his assistant put a stick in the ground and measured the length of its shadow. Using trigonometry they worked out the sun's distance from the earth. I thought about it for a moment, then asked "Since it was ancient times and they had no phones or radios, how did they know to do it at the same time?" He blinked. He must have stood for five minutes thinking. The class began talking amongst themselves. "Ah! Yes." he exclaimed "they were on the same latitude. In other words they knew which day they would do the experiment on and the measurement was taken at midday. The assistant was probably directly north of the well" I'm sure he was pleased to find the answer; and delighted to know knowledge wasn't accepted blindly like scriptures from a holy book. Radiation was one of his subjects. Radioactive sources were of course regarded as dangerous, each packaged in a little lead lined box. They were removed from the box using long probes so the handler did not get too close. He demonstrated how the boxes and probes worked. Opening a box, and using a probe, he showed the sample to us, finally replacing it in the box. He closed the lid. Using a Geiger counter around the sides, he showed how effective the lining was. Smiling, he looked up, "Things are not always what they seem" turning the box over he pointed the Geiger counter at the bottom, it went wild. "It is always worth checking things out for yourself. It turns out there is no protection underneath. You'll notice I always pick up the boxes by their sides"

The other excellent Physics teacher was Pat Jennings. He looked like the archetypal mad professor with wild hair and matching moustache, keen on astronomy and Einstein type physics. He explained how two atomic clocks were set to the same time. One on a plane and flown around the world; the other remained on the ground. The times were compared, they showed a difference. The one on the plane was now ahead of the one on the ground. He explained the one flown around the world had travelled at high speed and would therefore have been more influenced by relativistic effects. He stopped and stared at the two figures, "That doesn't make sense" he muttered, he looked again at the results. Pausing for a while, then continued muttering. Eventually he said "Ah! Of course. The results are correct. The one on the plane was in a weaker gravitational field than the one on the ground". He explained what happened. To me, the most interesting thing is, when others have given the same information, most claimed the figures had been mixed up and published the wrong way round. Personally the physics world should be proud of two such teachers as Mr. Postlethwaite and Pat Jennings.

For a few months we had a physics student-teacher, who will remain nameless. He was normally present as an assistant. One day Pat Jennings was away so the student-teacher took the lesson. It was about colloids. Stuff like clouds, salad cream and other weird substances which are not normal solid, liquid or gas. Towards the end of the lesson he asked "Why are clouds grey?" Several members of the class raised their hands "Yes" he said, pointing to Sebastian "Its pollution sir", "Yes, you're right" Everyone was aware he was an avid ecologist and environmentalist. This is nonsense; the reason clouds are grey is simply because of the shadows they make. Thunder clouds can be black because they are so thick and the shadows more noticeable. The world of physics should be ashamed of such a person passing convenient, inaccurate and thoughtless information as knowledge.

Shyness, and timidity were still part of life as a teenager. As with many teenage boys it was difficult to interact with girls, certainly on a sexual level. Words would fail me, as though frozen, a part of the process waiting for something to happen. It was actually difficult to interact with anyone. No one seemed to think like I did, or see the world in the same way. The people I got on with best often came from abroad, in some cases English was their second language. Looking back many gay people relate a similar experience of feeling different and alienated. I'm not gay, but the similarity is striking. Sleep also changed during my teen years. There was a period of about six weeks when sleep was only an hour and a half a night. Walking around the town at night gave some relief from the internal pressures. Terrible night sweats developed at this time. These would not stop until getting out of bed and standing up, sheets were usually sodden, something which still happens. Somewhere during teen years another change started to appear. Whilst dreaming about a person, part way through the dream I would realise they were someone else. The recognition would be immediate, and the dream would alter accordingly. The people concerned could be different colours, ages, builds; visually they would not be easy to mistake for one another. Dark, and normal dreams, still happened, though don't remember any in particular from that time; dreams have always been an escape, even when they have been terrifying; or rather, especially when they have been terrifying.

From about the age of ten I suffered night cramps. As a teenager these became worse. They would occur in the legs, mostly the left one. It was painful, and felt like there was a knot in the muscle for up to a week afterwards. The only way to deal with it was get up. In my mid-teens the same cramp would occur when swimming. By eighteen years old swimming stopped. Cramp would happen in other parts of limbs, though legs were the worst. Once cramp struck the top and bottom of a leg. It was an effort to put weight on it and relax at the same time.

In 1977, a teacher approached me about making up numbers for the rifle club. The club was due to take part in a competition that evening and one of the group was ill. Agreeing, but pointed out other than the fairground I had no experience of rifles or shooting. It was fine, only the highest scores would count towards the points, it was just to make sure the team numbers were correct. The range was 25 metres; we were each given 15 bullets. 5 for target practice to adjust the sights, the remaining 10 for the actual targets. I was nervous, and dismayed to see how small the targets were. Embarrassingly taking twice as long to shoot as the rest of the group. When targets were recovered the group was astonished, my score 97.8%, was the highest score not just of the group, but the county. The army, who were in charge of the range felt nervousness made me shift my body around, which lined up each shot. Even though the team came second in the competition, that evening I became county champion.

My appetite has always been big, and to the exasperation of others, not put weight on. As a teenager fondness developed for tonic water; gin was not added for several years. Around the same time hot baths started, to the point where I would be bright pink.

Learning foreign languages was enjoyable, though unsuccessful. For my third year Susan Caro taught French. An attractive, gentle young woman, teaching with kindness and understanding. She was going blind. The retinas in her eyes were damaged. When talking with someone she appeared to be looking somewhere completely different. First meeting her was always disconcerting, but being a nice person most people accepted her odd stare quickly. It must have been lonely and frightening. She taught French in an unusual style for the time. One lesson of the week was devoted to speaking French only, no English to be used. It was refreshingly different and her attitude was positive. We all knew it would be her last year, the encroaching blindness had become too much. On the last week of the final term there were no lessons, exams dominated. It was late afternoon in the language lab. I walk softly so she was unaware of me at the open door, whilst sorting papers at her desk. There was an intense desire to go up, kneel down, hug, and say everything would be alright. I didn't, unable to. Walking away after a minute. One of those regrets in life, a moment lost when comfort could have been given to someone who desperately needed it.

Chapter 3: Adulthood

I have always been aware of my heartbeat and breathing; it is surprising so many people are not. In swimming and yoga my breath control is considered excellent. Once in a while my heart jumps, like a sledgehammer hitting the inside of the chest. Often wondering how real it was, or just an overactive imagination. Once, stood embracing a close friend, she rested her head on my chest, for maybe a minute. My heart thumped. She pulled her head back sharply staring, "My god Ian! What is that? It's really strong". At times when my heart jumps there has been a strange sensation. In later years it has become more distinct, and is best described as "someone reading over your shoulder". Talking to one of my half-brothers about it, he said "I get that! That's exactly what it's like. You've got me thinking now". In medical terms, this is a panic attack.

Anita and I met at work in 1982, we married two years later. I was present at the birth of our children, Angelica 1986 and Glenda 1989. Angelica's birth was memorable for several reasons. The doctor was marvellous, but stretched running back and forth from different rooms looking after several pregnancies. The nurses and mid-wife would have performed caesarean, if left to their own devices, more for their CV's than the good of Anita and our unborn child. The doctor knew what they were discussing behind his back, and insisted Anita, using stirrups, could manage without caesarean. He was right, she did. Angelica was awake and aware from the moment of her birth. Big blue eyes looked at everything, turning her head to look around the room, staring at me for a moment. She drank everything in before being given to Anita.

I was a doting Dad, carrying them facing inwards in a sling on my front. There were many sniggers from my family who felt 'Mum' should have been my title. Both of our children spoke later than normal. Anita was concerned so we visited a child psychologist about Angelica. The psychologist explained it was not unusual for late speech development, however, it was usually amongst twins and not in a single child. The psychologist said, Angelica was developing her own language and should be forced to use English instead. We ignored the advice since, as a general principle, I was never keen on being forced by others, and saw no reason why Angelica would like it either. She learnt to speak in her own good time. Her ability to mimic others later in life was excellent, often with humorous results. When Glenda showed the same reluctance to talk, again we visited a psychologist. This time though Anita was more relaxed about it.

We travelled to visit Anita's family in the Philippines in 1989 when Glenda was six months old. They were delighted to see us. There were several social parties and gatherings. Filipinos speak English, but when talking with each other tend to drop into one of many dialects, it never bothered me. I feel little difference at social gatherings whether English is spoken or not. In the UK I live in London and tend not to have contact with animals, in the Philippines an oddity came up which had been forgotten about. I had a strong desire to bark and growl at dogs, not in an angry way, but almost conversationally.

One night we were asleep, Angelica was in the cot next to us. I became aware of a tall dark figure at the end of the bed. The figure was 7 feet tall and broad. It came closer, I tried to get up, and couldn't move. Terror and panic overwhelmed me. In that instant I thought about Angelica. Determined to stop this figure who felt so threatening; taking an enormous deep breath and shouting as loud and hard as possible. Anita, Angelica and I woke with a start. The shout had been real, the figure a dream, though it felt real. Not a moment to be forgotten.

During my adult life dreaming continued. A particular one is falling from what feels like five miles high. It's almost impossible to breathe, pressure on my chest is intense, and the air is cold, falling faster and faster. The ground looms up, and about fifteen feet before hitting it all the momentum shifts into speeding along horizontally. Concentrating and relaxing at the same time, if this weird state of mind is held I can control the direction of movement. Usually flying over sunlit countryside, jumping hedges and following the contour of the land. Initially the dream terrified me. After several occurrences I decided to try and enjoy it. From then on it was fantastic, something to look forward to. People were disturbed when listening to the description of the dreams so I rarely discussed them with anyone, including Anita who is religious and superstitious.

As well as dreams, night sweats continued. Sweating would not stop until getting out of bed. Sheets soaked as though from a washing machine. Anita, not surprisingly, was uncomfortable with it, often complaining of its peculiarity. Nothing seemed to cause it, nor did it follow a pattern.

As a child I learnt to play chess, badly as it turned out. By the mid-eighties the chess playing had improved, lazy when playing colleagues at work; making weak moves, certain they would still work against those opponents. A sign of over confidence, if ever there was. Playing one particular man, Raphael, in a corner of the stalls bar. Laziness was not an option with him, he was good enough to win. Thinking carefully when playing, sometimes a cold sensation travelled down under my left arm, presumably just a nervous reaction. Once so distinct, glancing down to my left hand sweat was running off the little finger. It only seemed to happen when motionless and thinking deeply.

Angelica and Glenda were bright, energetic children. They loved swimming, Anita would drive to Edmonton Green once a week across the North Circular road when it was being re-built (yet again) to make sure they attended lessons. They were excellent swimmers understanding to reach their arms far ahead and flow through the water. One of the instructors noted Glenda was exceptional. He said

"When she starts the lesson, she's just like everyone else. But by the end of it when the rest of them are flagging, you'd think she'd just arrived, not at all out of breath". It was ironic because from almost two years old she suffered severe asthma until her late teens. Her first asthma attack was late autumn 1990. It was a fresh cold morning, we were walking to Angelica's school. On the last part of the walk Angelica was encouraging Glenda to race against her. Angelica stayed just ahead whilst Glenda ran to keep up. She suddenly stopped, turning round to look at me, white and unable to breathe. She held out her arms to be picked up. Rising into the air turning to look at Angelica still running ahead blissfully unaware. Glenda pointed in her direction I obligingly jogged to catch up. The only concern was to catch her sister. We got Angelica to school. I carried Glenda home. She had not been upset or disturbed by the episode. After a second episode we took her to the GP who diagnosed asthma.

The asthma was so severe at times she did not have breath to register on the peak flow meter, a device used to measure breath strength. We would go straight to hospital for treatment. In all those years she suffered attacks, never once passing out; remaining calm all the time and not fighting it. When she was six, during an attack I drove her to hospital, she turned to me and said in gasping breathes "Daddy, I like it, when you drive. You always, calm me down". As a parent it is wonderful to hear your child say such a thing.

Like many people I enjoy computer games. One day 'Chip's Challenge' was being played on the backroom computer. Glenda watched through the double doors from the kitchen. After half an hour. "Dad", "Yes", "You're beginning to scare me. Do you know you've been playing for at least twenty minutes and haven't blinked once?" I stopped. She was right. Thinking about it further I had always been able to control my blinking. In 1988 at work a customer panicked and sprayed a member of staff with CS gas whilst in the bar. The bar immediately cleared with people unable to stay, tears streaming down their faces. The gas floated to the bar below, that also cleared. Raphael told me what was happening, I went to deal with the customer. I recall being cross and demanding to know why he thought it was OK to do such a thing. I was the only person unaffected by the gas. Looking back, it was probably due to my annoyance, being so focussed on the culprit and not blinking my eyes.

Angelica and Glenda are level-headed and able to keep calm at times of stress. When Angelica was four years old, she, Anita and Glenda were in the front room watching television. The smoke detector went off in the corridor. Glenda started crying, Anita felt her heart jump and didn't know what to do. Angelica opened the door to the corridor, ran to the kitchen, opened its door, looked in, closed the door, ran back and calmly said "Mummy. Your cooking's burning". Anita dealt with the burnt food and told me what happened later. She could not believe how calm Angelica had been. Both daughters have been in situations where others have panicked and flapped, but they have remained calm and dealt with the problem. They are looked to by others for help or guidance.

By mid-forties varicose veins in my legs had become severe and needed treatment. The left leg was treated first. I was given a local anaesthetic and wheeled into the operating theatre. An attractive nurse chatted to me as a distraction. Several students watched the operation, it took about fifteen minutes. At one point the entire operating theatre came to a standstill whilst staring at the leg in a manner suggesting a horror film was unfolding. The surgeon talked to the students all this time and at one point said "… eleven point four." as he described a vein. The attractive nurse looked at me and said "That would be what we call a 'juicy one'." The operation was initially successful, though in November 2014 the same leg had to be treated again. A year after the first operation the right leg was treated. The surgeon met me before surgery and talked about what would happen. He apologised for not recognising me, and wasn't sure if we had met before, he performed so many operations and could never remember people. I smiled and said "Eleven point four". He flinched, "Oh god! You had stonking great veins". I still don't know what eleven point four means, it is obviously a medical term for 'stonking great'.

I am kind-hearted by nature and a complete pacifist. There have been violent situations, but never been able to hurt anyone, even when others would say it was justified. One of my greatest pleasures in life is helping others, even total strangers. A long-time friend, Norma, who referred to herself as my mother, once commented "Ian, you have the biggest heart of anyone I've met. I've learnt so much from you". Norma had spent most of her life helping other people, so it was a huge compliment.

Occasionally I have locked eyes with a woman. Finding myself in position where it is an effort for either of us to wrench away. It happened as recently as 2013. The woman was sat in a restaurant 'The Orange Tree' in Loughton with a group of friends. It only lasted a few seconds, but was an intense, enjoyable moment. It is usually with strangers, though has happened with someone I know, albeit slightly. An acquaintance at work, Federica, had a friend visit for a few weeks. Fede' introduced her to everyone at work and she would pop in during the evening to visit Fede'. On the night before returning to Italy, she was in the foyer. Fede' and her boyfriend were stood by the front doors, a few other people were around. I glanced up, my eyes locked with her friend's. For an eternal moment she was the most beautiful face. Eyes dark and wide in an innocent stare. Her nose and mouth made her look like a gazelle. I thought "This is rude of me", "I don't care. She looks so beautiful and this is a moment to remember" Drinking in everything possible I have no idea how long we stood like that. It was probably about 40 seconds, it felt like forever. Hopefully it was as enjoyable for her as it was for me. Years later I apologised to Fede for any embarrassment. She merely smiled and said "She's married now".

I met Jane in November 2004, group interviews were held for front of house positions for the opening of 'Mary Poppins'. Four of us conducted the interviews. The groups were each of ten people. Jane was in one of those groups. It was impossible to take my eyes off her. She was beautiful, charismatic, vivacious and intelligent. Years later when we talked I said none of those words did her justice; it was more like meeting the goddess of electricity for the first time. Several times during the interview I closed my eyes to tear them away.

We became good friends. She was always energetic and smiling. She left after a few months, but would come back to visit me. She is tactile and genuinely enjoys hugging. It was a lovely surprise to discover she gives the best hug ever; even today I have not been hugged by anyone as deeply as Jane. We began to meet every couple of months to talk and get a bite to eat, often in an ice cream parlour in Leicester Square. She would relate all the things she'd been up to, boyfriends, social life. When we were in the parlour she preferred to sit upstairs, and would order ice cream and drinks. Most times I would have the chocolate drink, which was extremely chocolaty, towards the end of which I would sometimes break out in sweat. It struck me often what a strange friendship it was. We had nothing in common, yet enjoyed each other's company, always parting with a hug. Both of us motionless for several seconds. For me the hug was the most important part of meeting her, an escape from the empty world. Over the years coincidences began to emerge. She would call me and would only be a couple of hundred yards away. One of the strangest coincidences, one afternoon whilst walking through China town my phone rang. "Hi!" I said "Hi! It's Jane." "How are you?" "I'm good, thanks. Just in China town" "Where in China town?" "I'm on Wardour Street" "Really! Where on Wardour street? I'm standing here now" "Well I'm not actually on Wardour street, I'm eating in a restaurant" She described it. Turning round and looking through the window behind me. Sure enough, she was sat in the back of the restaurant on her phone, oblivious to me at the window. I would also often know if a text was from her before looking at the phone.

Around 2008/2009 Anita and I were asleep in bed. There was a dark, shadowy figure at the bottom of the stairs outside our bedroom. The bedroom seemed different. The armchair was lit by sunlight as it streamed through what seemed like two windows. I woke up taking large deep gasping breathes, so much so my chest was thrusting high whilst struggling to get air. Anita was crouched on a corner of the bed staring, terrified "What are you doing? I thought you were dying" I replied "I have no idea". We were both shocked and stunned, nothing like this had happened to me before. Strange things in my sleep were not unusual, but this was darker, and scarier. Shaken, we went back to sleep. There was a dark, shadowy figure at the bottom of the stairs outside our bedroom. The bedroom seemed different. The armchair lit by sunlight.... Anita was shaking and pushing me "You're doing it again" I was tired, rolled over going back to sleep. There was a dark, shadowy figure at the bottom of the stairs outside our bedroom. Anita pushed at me "You're doing it again" I went back to sleep. My mobile phone rang at about 5am. It was Jane, she was on holiday in Thailand with her boyfriend. They had run into difficulty and she was asking for help. Anita would normally be jealous of a woman calling me, but this time she was so shaken by what happened, other than to ask who had rung she said nothing about the call. The nightmare was disturbing, but because it was on the same night Jane rang, it meant not having to deal with jealousies or accusations of infidelity. It left me drained for about five weeks afterwards. I didn't tell Jane about the dreams and didn't discuss any of the coincidences with her, though at times she mentioned them. I forgot about the incident after a few months, our friendship was good and there seemed no need to try and make anything of it.

Jane and I were having coffee and ice cream in Leicester Square when she told me she was emigrating with her boyfriend. My heart sank "I will miss you a great deal. I love you very much. But, if you're going, you're going". We continued talking about what she was doing and her hopes for emigration. Afterwards we walked out into Leicester square, at one point she became cheeky with me. I said "I don't want to go that way" referring to her flirting "I still want to know you in ten years' time" She didn't speak, but in her head clearly said "That isn't going to happen". I have been aware of people's thoughts before, this time was clear and strong. It hurt and was depressing. I said nothing.

In June 2010 Anita and I started divorce proceedings. I slept on the floor of the downstairs backroom until able to purchase somewhere else. It was not an amicable split, tense and difficult all round. So many things seemed to go wrong. The mortgage offer from a building society, withdrawn two months after being given. A new mortgage with a bank was made. The first property taken from the market a few weeks after accepting the offer. Apparently the seller was merely testing the market. The second property was turned down at the last minute by the bank, even though initially they approved it. The third property was gazumped on the day contracts were due to be exchanged. In October my solicitor commented "I do hope this brings an end to your run of bad luck" The fourth property kept experiencing delays until February 2011 with long frustrating silences from both vendor and estate agent. The completion date was continually pushed back. The mortgage expiry loomed. In a busy house the backroom floor was a lonely place to be; at least my back stopped aching. One day before the mortgage offer was due to expire on 28th March 2011 completion and moving happened. The solicitor expressed surprise at my patience and endurance knowing the divorce was happening as well. A couple of years later a work colleague said he saw me during this time, walking down a street head bowed, bent over, trudging, carrying the world on my shoulders; looking haggard and old. He felt sad, but couldn't bring himself to go up and talk with me.

When the move came most things were left behind, including the car. Too expensive to run, there was no point in having it. I missed driving, it was therapeutic and relaxing. Within a few months of moving into the new place it was evident my children wanted nothing to do with me. Texts and calls brought no response. I am neither gregarious nor outgoing. Despite working in London's West End have never enjoyed a vibrant social life. Because of the marital difficulties it was hard to stay in contact with joint friends, or Anita's family. It caused anxieties for her with conflicting loyalties and awkwardness. Mum and Kim each came to see me once, otherwise there were no visitors for the first 18 months after moving in. Divorce proceedings continued for a year after the move until the papers came through on February 14th 2012; it is fair to say my solicitor possesses a sense of humour. For a long time my soul ran on 'empty'.

After completing the move there was a determination not to collapse, and to embrace life. Every day included a walk around the new neighbourhood. There are many different races and cultures in London's East End, it has wonderful variety. A stranger in a strange land, it was to be a great adventure. I had been so pleased to get a three bedroom duplex. The extra bedrooms meant either of the girls could stay with me if they needed. For the first few weeks I slept in the downstairs backroom. There was a radio and laptop for company. The nearby second-hand office equipment shop, also sold cheap carpet tiles. As and when budget allowed, tiles and furniture were bought. I continued sleeping on the floor until 2013; it was good for my back and helped control the sciatica.

On 12th August 2011 Jane flew to Thailand. Her grandmother was seriously ill. I was off work from the 15th for a couple of weeks, decorating and trying to get the new place up to scratch, it was run down and neglected. Part of the break was trying fun new things, such as wall murals, watercolours, card making. There was little contact with other people then, the situation imposed solitude. The only regular contact was a daily phone call to Mum. On Wednesday 24th a work colleague who lives a few bus stops away, should have visited, but cancelled at the last minute; another day on my own. The only trip out was to the local supermarket, treating myself to a pack of mini pork pies. The intention had been decorating, the reality, Facebook. The evening was spent chatting online to a friend in the US until late, eventually falling asleep in the smallest bedroom just before 2am.

There was a dark figure, bottom of the stairs outside the bedroom. Hard to make out if it was one large figure, or two, a smaller one stood behind the first. The bedroom was 'the wrong way round'. I was lying on what felt like a metal framed single bed with curved ends. Enormous deep gasping breathes woke me; chest thrusting high in the air. It was bewildering. Checked the time on the mobile phone. Twenty past two. Neighbours were noisy next door, maybe they'd woken me? Went back to sleep.

Was a dark figure at bottom of stairs outside bedroom? Hard to make out if it was one large figure, or two, a smaller one stood behind taller one. The bedroom was 'the wrong way round'. Lying on what felt like a metal framed single bed with curved ends. Enormous deep gasping breathes woke me, chest thrusting high in the air. Checked time. Twenty to three. Disturbing. Maybe pork pies I'd eaten? Went to sleep.

A dark figure at bottom of stairs outside room. Hard to make out if it was one large figure, or two, a smaller one stood behind taller one. Bedroom 'wrong way round'. Lying on what felt like a metal frame bed with curved ends. Enormous deep gasping breathes woke me, chest thrusting high in air. Checked mobile. 3 o'clock. Wondered, the weird bed. Draining. Slept...

Dark figure at bottom of stairs outside room. Hard to make out if it was one large figure, or two, a smaller one stood behind taller one. Bedroom 'wrong way round'. Lying on what felt like a metal frame bed with curved ends. Enormous deep gasping breathes woke me, chest thrusting high in air. Time check. 3:20 a.m. Scary. Could I die? Violence of waking. Frightening. Slept…

Dark figure at bottom of stairs outside room. Hard to make out if one large figure, or two, a smaller one stood behind taller one. Bedroom 'wrong way round'. Lying on what felt like metal frame bed. Enormous deep gasping breathes woke me, chest thrusting high in air. Check mobile. 3:40. Tired. So, tired. Sleep…

Dark figure at bottom of stairs outside room. Hard to make out, one large figure, or two, a smaller one behind taller one. Bedroom 'wrong way round'. Lying on single bed. Deep gasping breathes woke me, chest thrusting high. 4 a.m. So tired. Die? Didn't care. Sleep…

Figure, bottom, stairs. Hard, make out, one figure, two. Bedroom 'wrong way round'. Lying, single bed. Deep gasping breathes, me, chest thrusting. 4:20. Sleep.

4:26a.m. phone rang. Jane. Terrible state. Grandmother in hospital. Nothing doctors could do. Slipping away. Jane desperate, get her out, get home. Not the place to die. In their last moments people should be surrounded by their nearest and dearest, at home. The hospital could not release her until bills were paid. They would not accept credit card, there was not enough money in my bank account. Tears ran down the inside of her nose as she talked. Despair flowed down the phone. All during the call there was a sinking feeling, of being swallowed into a tar pit. The next hour and a half was spent ringing banks and credit card providers to see what could be done, all to no avail, frustration filled me. At quarter past six Jane sent a text explaining she had the money and not to worry. Barriers broke. The floodgates did not close that day.

The next day she put a message on Facebook saying grandmother had died. I had not slept. I sent a text message, the first two verses from 'Make you feel my love' since they felt so right to her situation, even the weather, at the end of the text it said 'nothing inappropriate meant'. Looking back she obviously misunderstood. Our friendship died in that instant. She distanced herself breaking off all contact over the next few weeks.

The nervous breakdown opened and crushed me, like being subdued and swallowed by a snake; yet also a typhoon, naked, shivering, and clinging to a wet rock for dear life. Some nights there would be two hours sleep, others, less. When sleep came it was not a relief, with vivid dreams and nightmares, the worst when dream thoughts were the same as waking thoughts, unable to let go of dread and anxiety. A whole nights' sleep did not happen until mid-October. The end of November, at last sleep came for the whole night, not leaving me feeling beaten up. Sleep normalised about a year after the call. For several weeks at work my door was closed, so colleagues would not see tears stream down my face. Outside the office they were almost controllable, on my own or in the street where only strangers walk, they flowed, especially on platforms waiting for trains. This went on until the end of 2012. Years later, in private, tears still occasionally visit. If they didn't, it would be a sign of cold-heartedness, it means there is life and feeling inside. Jane never knew what happened to me. There was no goodbye, a special friend, irreplaceable, possibly unique; gone.

Chapter 4: Specialist Help

Have always been suspicious of experts in psychology and mental health. It often seems treatment is for the problem they wish you had. Initially I did not seek treatment. A few people at work knew what happened to me, but on the whole it was kept from everyone else. The interior decorating stopped completely. All work at home stalled. Unsurprisingly the artwork reflected my mood. It didn't help with getting better, it did show the feelings inside. The technical side of art, 3d drawings, scale and perspective had always been there. Now dark emotion showed through.

At the end of September 2011 I visited Wendy, Dad's sister, in Corfu for a week. We hadn't seen each other for fourteen years, it was good to meet. We talked in the evenings, mostly about the time she lived in Banbury. At one point she observed Dad had never loved anyone, not even himself. We went swimming most days in the sea. Sleep was still fleeting. The flight back to Gatwick was on 1st October. On landing there was a Facebook message from Jane to everyone in the UK. She was emigrating that day. In arrivals I sat and cried.

On 8th October the local gym in Ilford was joined for swimming, something neglected over the last thirty years. For a month one mile a day was the average. Swimming underwater gave the best relief. I can swim underwater for 25 metres with one breathe. It is a combination of focussing on the task in hand and staying relaxed, 'mindless' and in the moment. It is wonderful being there. Voices and noises are muted. It is clear and fresh in my head. Of all things for beating back tears and sadness, swimming was the most effective. To swim underwater for a length of the pool a pause is needed, letting the heartbeat get back to normal. Look down the lane, take a breath, dive underwater and swim. One evening the dive underwater was miss-timed. It hurt my chest, like having a lump in the throat. Normally my pulse is fifty plus beats a minute. On this occasion the pulse was ninety plus. It stayed high all night. By morning it was back to normal, a little scary.

In mid-November yoga was taken up to improve my social life, none of the other activities at the gym were appealing. It deals with strength, flexibility and balance; both physical and mental. There are postures and exercises to do, each of which has an associated way of breathing. The first time practising a particular breathing exercise was enlightening, but not the way the teacher indicated. We were told to stand, relax, and let the arms hang by our sides. Close the eyes and breathe in gently through our nostrils. Further instructions on what to do were given. I don't recall them, as soon as my eyes closed, it was a different world. Impossible to think about the breathing. I felt like a wriggling fish, with the wriggles starting from the chest. It felt in some ways similar to swimming underwater. Every time the breathing exercise was tried it happened, but over months becoming less intense. By March / April 2012 the 'wriggling fish' stopped. It happened to me a couple of years later after a minor incident which upset me. This time when it hit my eyes sprang open, breathed in, relaxed, closed the eyes, and it was gone. It seems it's directly related to anxiety.

At times in yoga my limbs, especially legs turned blue. This concerned everyone else more than it did me being used to it in cold weather. One of the yoga teachers, Maggie, ends her classes with us lying down face up, eyes closed and relaxed in 'corpse' pose. She then reads a short story, usually about our perceived imperfections, emotions and how we relate to the world. For the first nine months tears would run down my face during those stories; it was a release, she has my lifelong gratitude. A believer in love and affection.

A work colleague advised me to seek psycho-therapy treatment; suggesting a clinic in Waterloo. Following her advice the treatment started in December 2011. At the initial interview, in October, everything about the night and phone call was related. The interviewer took notes and asked me to relate early childhood memories. At the one about Dad saying "Why can't you eat quietly?" tears rolled down my cheeks. The interviewer sympathised and felt this was the real problem. Every week talking with the psycho-therapist, he wished to concentrate on childhood memories and was interested in neither the call nor the aftermath. By December most nights I was waking by 4am; sometimes to sweats, often with my hair and face drenched, or at times trying to vomit. December 21st was a tear-stained night, duvet-wrapped in a corner of the bedroom. The next day I recalled Jane had rung during the night once before. "Why didn't Anita go mad at me?" Recollection flooded back, it was because she had been so terrified by my 'seizures' on that night. It came up in discussion at the next psycho-therapy session. After five minutes of talking without any comment from the psycho-therapist he tried directing the conversation to childhood experiences. After a few weeks I stopped the psycho-therapy sessions, any improvements had nothing to do with treatment. At the time of the initial interview I was upset, a discussion about the rules of draughts would have made tears flow. To decide it was my childhood now looks presumptuous and, manipulative.

From 2012 to 2014 time was spent thinking about what happened; contacting relevant institutions and professionals, using the letter which follows; plus another one based on the thoughts in Chapter 5. The letter has not been changed from its original form.

A sixth sense

I have had an experience, or more accurately two pairs of experiences that have forced me to conclude there is a communication sense that is neither visual, chemical nor *aural; it seems to be a very real genuine physiological sense and not one that is properly documented.*

In 2008/2009 I was asleep in bed with my wife. There was a presence on the staircase outside of our bedroom. I awoke and realised I had been taking deep rapid breathes, possibly four or five that I could recall. My wife was crouched on the other side of the bed staring at me and said "I thought you were dying. What's wrong with you?" I replied that I didn't know and we both went back to sleep. Later that night I had the same dream of someone on the staircase and found my wife waking me up saying "You're doing it again", I realised once again I had been taking in deep rapid breathes. At about 5a.m. I received a phone call from a very close friend. I cannot remember the exact problem, but they needed help and were quite upset. The details are very sketchy from that time.

The night of August 24th/25th 2011 I went to bed at 2a.m. and fell asleep immediately. I became aware of a shadowy figure on the stairs, though sometimes it felt like two figures. I was lying on a bed (in actuality I sleep on the floor), the room felt the wrong way round. Upon waking up I became aware of taking deep rapid breathes, maybe four or five in about two seconds. I looked at the time then went back to sleep. The same dream with the rapid breathing kept recurring during the night with a gap of about twenty minutes between each until at 4:26 a.m. I received an extremely distressed phone call from the same friend who was in desperate need of help.

The friend in question has only rung me during the night on those two occasions. That I am aware of I have not had the experience and excessive breathing on any other night. In both cases the call was not expected, my friend was in Thailand, I was in London. I do not believe in sorcery and can only conclude that somehow or other her emotional state was conveyed to me on those occasions. The second call in occurrence in particular left me extremely disturbed for many months. This may simply be an overreaction.

The letter was written as coldly and objectively as possible so as to stick with facts. There have been no responses from any medical institutions. The few responses from what might be called 'pseudoscience', did not offer any useful advice or suggestions. A small number of targeted individuals did answer, but no one contributed anything useful and none were interested in discussing it further, with one exception.

What happened to me was an occurrence of Extra Sensory Perception, or ESP. By March 2012 an idea formed as to how it happened in terms of physiology. The search for medical knowledge and help continued, my doctor, after hearing everything, said "Ah! Yes! Some people are sensitive like that. You need to see a psychologist". The first psychologist was thrown by it and freely admitted so, having never encountered anything like this. By the end of the interview she decided to pass it onto a senior colleague, George, more experienced and able to help. George listened and asked questions about other dreams and started to focus on childhood events. He was annoyed when I would not drop the subject of what happened to me, becoming angry and sarcastic "Well, if you want my opinion, you're heading for a nervous breakdown.", "What are you going to do about all this anger?", "The incident is irrelevant, and has nothing to do with it. Anyway, how are you going to prove it?" There seemed no point in saying he was predicting the past, or in asking why proof was needed. In the report he wrote of our meeting, he said nothing of the things I talked about. My GP's report also did not mention the night Jane rang other than to say "The patient has bad dreams".

The exceptional response was Professor David at a College, ironically he is an ESP sceptic. He agreed to a twenty minute talk, it stretched to more than thirty. Even though we didn't agree, he was a breath of fresh air compared to the few previous responses and opinions. He thought my suggestion was unique, but said, "The problem you have with me is simply I don't believe in ESP" He was taken aback when asking if Rupert Sheldrake, a leading parapsychologist, had been contacted. I sighed "He responded with 'interesting theory' and went on to say how marvellous his own work was". David said it wouldn't be taken seriously, because researchers studying the phenomena already had funding in place, and would not drop their current study in favour of my suggestion.

It was disappointing to find the medical world was unhelpful and actually in some cases, stupid. For months inside I was screaming, pounding on walls to be heard. To no avail, no one listened, no one cared to. Specialist help was no help at all. Despite the despair they inspired, I did not give up, the book began.

Chapter 5: Whoa! What just happened?

The dreams, breathing fits and the phone calls during those two nights were not coincidence. It seems Jane subconsciously sent a 'natural' distress call which triggered the fits. Before working out what happened, we should look at the other senses, including animal ones, to see how nature works in this respect.

Sight is our most powerful and prominent sense accounting for 83% of sensory input. Information pours into us at an astonishing rate, it would flood a super computer in seconds. It gives detail, shape, distance, movement, speed and colour. The distance is limited by the curvature of the earth, the transparency of the atmosphere (foggy days we hardly see any distance) and objects blocking the view. The range of light is limited, starting from red through to blue. The higher and lower frequencies are invisible to us. We are aware of seeing through our eyes and they are placed at an ideal viewing point in the front of our heads. Sight gives information about immediate events and environment in front of us.

Hearing is the second major sense accounting for 11% of sensory input. It can give distance, direction and movement, though to a lesser degree than seeing. Alterations in sound give complex understanding of our environment, we can tell the difference between a bell and breaking glass, and know when someone is calling our name. There are noises from objects and sounds from ourselves and other animals. The healthy human hearing range is 20Hz to 20,000Hz, as adults we tend to lose the extremes of this. Sensitivity to the human voice is greater than any other part of the spectrum. Hearing in some ways is more complex than seeing since we make noises ourselves. The ears, nose and throat are all connected, allowing us to hear ourselves, whilst listening to other sounds. It is difficult, but this is how choirs can sing in unison, and why medical specialists in this field study the ears, nose and throat. Hearing is awareness of our surroundings; human voices, and music convey emotional states and interaction. When we talk to each other only 7% of the message is the meaning of words, everything else is made up of tones, inflections, rhythm, etc... How we sound is more important than what we say, as actors and politicians know.

The sense of touch is about 3.5% of sensory input. Touch is immediate, requiring contact with the particular surface or object. There is more than one type of touch, hot, cold, pain, texture, pressure, to name some. Your body deals with these all the time, mostly you are unaware of it, unless you are wearing a particularly itchy shirt. The sub-conscious deals with this, along with the sense of balance and muscle feedback allowing us to move around, even clamber over rocks whilst wearing clothes and shoes. Touch with other people is intimate, even the slightest touch can change our dealings with others dramatically, and alter perceptions of them.

1.5% of our sensory world is through smell. For each of us smell has the capacity to evoke memories; barbecues, flowers, trips abroad and such-like. On a negative note we learn to ignore our own body odour, which others may find offensive. Many senses are able cut out our own interference: Other than people with damaged nerve endings it is next to impossible for most of us to tickle our own feet.

At a conscious level taste is pure self-indulgence, though only 1% of our senses. It works best in unison with smell, but hearing, touch and sight also contribute. Did you know wine tastes better in a heavy glass? It is about pleasure, our ability to taste poisons is zero. It is involved in cravings for certain foods with specific chemicals, rather than just the standard fats, sugars, hydro-carbons and proteins. Pregnant women often get cravings for particular foods, even if they don't like them.

The percentage figures given are approximate and vary amongst experts. They are there to give a sense of proportion. Balance is not usually listed among the senses even though we all possess it. Like taste, balance works best in unison with other senses, eyesight, touch and muscle feedback. Unlike most senses we are not aware of the balance organ itself, located in the inner ear. The sense of balance cannot be blocked, though it can be confused. We all remember a time stepping off the fairground ride and a continual falling over feeling.

Unsurprisingly, animals are different from us. All the senses listed occur in other animals with a greater range and sensitivity. If a man and his dog stand at the edge of a field looking across countryside. The man may see beautiful flowers, hear birds singing and take in the smell of freshly mown hay. Dogs are colour blind, so no beautiful flowers for him, yet will catch the slightest movement. He will hear birds singing, and also things that escape our human ears, insects, the sounds of breathing, movements of other animals. Aside from hay he will smell animals which have passed by, and from scent alone know how long since they did. For dogs smell is a narrator telling a story.

Each animal species, even individual members of a species may perceive the world differently. There are several types of colour-blindness, mostly in men, giving different views in our most significant sense. It is useful, colour-blindness reduces the effect of camouflage. Some insects see ultraviolet radiation, their view of flowers is still beautiful, but like glowing beacons. Vipers see infrared heat radiating from a body. They do so using a pit below the eye. This allows them to strike at the hottest blood vessels. Most people have heard of the remarkable ability of dogs and other animals to smell just a few molecules of a substance.

Some animals possess senses we don't seem to have. Bats hear and produce hypersonic sounds in the same way we use radar or echolocation. Pigeons sense magnetic lines, robins see them, but only with their right eye. Many of us know some fish and especially sharks sense electricity in the bodies of others nearby. It is not unique to sea creatures, the platypus detects tiny electric fields generated by muscle contractions when searching for food in muddy water. Presumably it has a system to stop its own fields interfering with this detection. There is a sensitivity to light which seems unique among the senses, it is in the pineal gland, part of the brain. In some sharks the skull is thin enough for this gland to respond to light. It appears to be the only case of a brain receiving direct sensory input.

There are two other senses possessed by snakes. You may be surprised to know they are deaf. So much for the snake charmers flute. They are able to sense vibrations in the ground through the lower jaw, which is composed of seven bones. A human jaw is made of one bone. We still possess the other six, they are in the middle ears transmitting sound vibrations to the inner ear. Nature doesn't usually scrap parts of the body, it adapts them, or in the case of the appendix shrinks and make them redundant. The other snake sense is Jacobsen's organ, located in the roof of its mouth. A snake flicks its tongue into the air to pick up particles, molecules, even pheromones. The tongue is drawn back into the mouth depositing these particles into Jacobsen's organ for 'tasting'. Because the snake's tongue is forked it tastes in stereo and can gain more information. It was discovered humans still possess this organ; it was presumed redundant like the appendix. Recently though doubt has been cast on this. It appears we are influenced by pheromones introduced to this organ, so a sense we are not aware of.

Returning to Jane's natural distress call. In her case, triggered by intense grief and anxiety. The signal travelled, presumably, as energy. The distance, at 6,000 miles is astonishing. Which organ, or organs, could send or receive such a signal. Finally, what was the signal saying?

Jane's state was extreme, anxious and upset, crying uncontrollably. Her brain was in an agitated state. Every organ affected and involved with this condition. The bloodstream filled with anxiety chemicals such as adrenaline. Skin, muscles, breathing and heart rate, all impacted, possibly sweating, definitely tears. That we know, humans are the only animal to cry tears of emotion Kidneys would be active. The entire nervous system, brain, spinal column and associated nerves were in a heightened state of activity. Stomach likely to have its functioning reduced along with other food digesting processes. Somewhere in Jane's body, amidst the chaos and turmoil, an organ sent a distress call.

Was the signal a general distress beacon or just to me? If aimed specifically at me, it seems unlikely to be directional, it would imply a permanent link or communication. There is no precedent for this in terms of communication between animals. Bat sonar is constant for monitoring the surrounding area, but only while flying. As soon as a bat lands it stops producing sonar. Most likely, between Jane and me, unknown to our conscious minds, there had been either an agreement or recognition of how messages such as this could be sent; a 'handshaking' protocol, in the form of energy, presumably as a pulse or pulses.

Energy forms we know of are light, sound, kinetic, chemical, electrical, radiation, magnetic and heat. For a person to be heard over 6,000 miles distance it would probably be louder than the eruption of Krakatoa. The loudest known animal is the blue whale, whose songs travel hundreds of miles and maybe the length of an ocean. Sound waves travel faster and better in water than air. In air it would have taken about 8 hours to travel 6,000 miles. Without even getting into any other obvious reasons, it cannot be sound.

Light emission is produced in animals naturally. It requires little energy, however there are no known examples of an animal being able to cast light any great distance. It appears limited to primitive life forms, jelly-fish, insects, etc... The curvature of the earth is a problem, even if the light were bright enough to travel the distance;

41

and the added difficulty of it being blocked by intervening objects. It will not be light, or if it is then far outside of the visible spectrum.

Chemicals, and chemical energy are not known for travelling and it seems impossible even for pheromones to have travelled the distance. Kinetic would suffer the same problems as sound, after all sound is just kinetic energy travelling in a substance. Heat would immediately be soaked up by the surrounding air and seems like a complete non-starter. This leaves radiation, electricity, magnetism or an undiscovered form of energy. There is no sign in nature any living creature has managed to make use of or control radiation. An alternative form seems unlikely, our knowledge of energy has remained constant for several decades with no apparent inconsistencies. This leaves magnetism and electricity.

There are electric and magnetic fields around the earth. The electric field is a potential difference in voltage as you rise up through the atmosphere, like the layers of an onion. The difference is about 120 volts per metre. The magnetic field also covers the entire planet. It flows from one pole to another, following similar lines to segments in an orange.

Any signal would be a ripple sent along the field rather than generating a new one, otherwise the energy required would be larger than we seem capable of. There are several creatures able to detect magnetism, cows and some deer graze in a north – south direction; possibly at a subconscious level it affects us. There doesn't appear to be any evidence of animals controlling magnetism. Electricity on the other hand, is one of the most common features of all life. Every living creature we know of produces an electric field. Several are known to detect electric fields, others able to control them. The more well known for giving shocks are sting rays and electric eels.

If the signal was along magnetic or electric fields, which organ was responsible for sending, and which for receiving? Assuming it's either electric or magnetic for the moment let's regard them as synonymous, they usually interact; the electric motor works because the two fields influence each other. The human body, like other animals, has electrical fields generated by individual organs. The brain, muscles, heart, and entire nervous system each have their own. The way our senses work, only one type of organ is responsible for receiving a particular sense, sometimes it's a pair of organs. For sending a signal it initially appears more complex. Ears, nose and throat are connected. Eyes are the most expressive part of our faces. It seems where a sense is in the position of receiving it is also involved or connected with sending. Therefore the organ which receives ESP is likely to be involved in sending. On the basis of electric fields in the human body there are only three serious contenders, heart, brain and spinal column.

Returning to the two nights when Jane rang the most significant aspects of each are the type of dream and the violent gasping breathes on waking. Presumably my breath was held in those last few moments of sleep. The brain has been extensively researched, which aside from the pineal gland, shows no sensory capability. The spinal column, an extension of the brain is responsible for many background functions. Again though it does not lend itself to being a sensory organ. The brain and spinal column are command centres which listen to the body and decide based upon what is heard. The lungs and heart work together as a team, between them they draw in the oxygen and propel it round the body. The heart has an electric field greater than the brain or spinal column. It is the strongest candidate for sending and receiving signals through the electric field. While my breath was being held, the heart was busy doing more than just pumping blood. Already there are a number of questions: Why isn't this happening to everybody all the time? Why don't other animals seem to have it? How exactly did it travel 6,000 miles? For the rest of the book it is assumed the heart is responsible for ESP.

Chapter 6: The Baby monitor

If the heart is able to send and receive electric signals, why would this happen and what are the consequences? The hearts main job is to pump blood. It does so twenty four hours a day for a lifetime; about two to three billion beats. If you lost your eyes, ears, sense of taste, smell or touch; life would be difficult, but you could live. If your heart, stops you die. There must be limits to how much the heart can deal with outside electrical signals, since its own are so vital. Eyes and ears have methods for dealing with increased intensity of light and sound, and still be able to detect low intensities. Even so, they can be damaged from over exposure. Arc welders' eye and deaf rock stars are common examples of this. There are several conditions a heart can have; some we are born with, others develop on life's journey. A hole in the heart is a birth defect, whereas many coronary diseases in the west are certainly excessive lifestyle.

The heart is a bag of muscle, divided into four chambers set as two pairs; a left, and a right pair. One takes blood from the body and sends it to the lungs, the other receives blood from the lungs and sends it round the body. The heart chambers are co-ordinated so the action of any one affects the performance and action of the others. Arrhythmia is where one chamber is out of sync with the rest, like a dancer out of step with their troupe; or a car engine where one cylinder is miss-firing. The heart can also be out of sync with the rest of the body. There are many types, and causes, not all of them understood. Below are characteristics for different arrhythmias which seem related to ESP. The last one is included since it is suspiciously similar to my physiology.

- Young females are often affected. Sometimes related to stress, fright, flight, anger or anxiety. Often requires no treatment.

- Some patients experience distressing symptoms, therapy may be necessary for reassurance. They may be inconsolable. It may be triggered by stress, or some foods, alcohol, strong cheese, chocolate. Often requires no treatment.
- There is a poor return of blood, it may pool in the legs. Often, people with this syndrome completely avoid salt during cooking and at the table.

Arrhythmias can be started by exertion, particularly swimming for one group, and also fear or excitement. Another group occurs during sleep. Many in young and fit people are 'Vagal' in origin. Vagal, or vagal tone, refers to the main part of the 'parasympathetic' system called the 'Vagus' nerve. It looks after the body's resting state and helps co-ordinate organs. Like a drummer in a modern band responsible for flow, rhythm and co-ordination of other musicians. High vagal tone is associated with adaptive or flexible living of a person; it usually reduces with age and poor health. It monitors the heartbeat, but is not simply a metronome. The task is complex, your heart beat changes during a breath in from a breath out; like waves on the seashore, rushing in yet flowing back. Vagal tone also regulates emotions and arousal, high vagal tone tends to give positive effects.

The information given about arrhythmias is selective and geared to the subject of this book. Specialist help should be sought for any problems, however, there is more to this than a mere medical complaint. Considering the seriousness of arrhythmia, it is surprising how many do not require treatment. I will say some arrhythmias are an interruption of the heartbeat caused by picking up a signal through the electric field from someone else.

Arrhythmia in pregnancy is the most interesting of all. It often occurs when there has been no history or underlying problem. Palpitations are common. In normal pregnancy the heart rate will increase by about 25%. Usually this type of arrhythmia is regarded as benign.

Given all we know about how remarkable mammal bodies are, is the mother's heart monitoring the baby's heartbeat, and therefore its health and well-being? A question springs to mind, why is it rare for a foetus to have arrhythmia? The mother's heart is going faster than normal, it has a large powerful electric field. Yet this tiny foetus growing inside of her, is oblivious to the pulsing dynamo above it, larger than its body. There is a major difference between their hearts. The foetus does not use its lungs; its heartbeat is different, because of the 'hole in the heart', there is no ebb and flow of air. The chamber sending blood to the lungs is not used. This may be a clue as to how the heart picks up, or sends an external electrical signal.

There seems to be similarities between cramps, arrhythmia and Raynauds. Cramp is often associated with salt deficiency and strenuous activity. The pain from one type of cramp can take up to a week to disappear. Other causes are reduced blood flow and de-hydration. Night cramps are known to cause distress and anxiety. As mentioned, arrhythmias can be connected to inconsolable anxiety, poor blood return where there is salt deficiency. It can be triggered by over-exertion or stress. Raynauds is restricted blood flow to extremities, especially the fingers, triggered by low temperatures or stress. For Raynauds my symptoms appear randomly and sometimes when practising yoga. Over the last few years the opposite effect is becoming noticeable, my hands will become scarlet, hot, and usually the skin is smooth and tight. It is unlikely these disorders are directly related, but the results of the same process or processes.

A mother cares for the infant inside of her body, supplying warmth and nutrition, chemical messages zip back and forth. Every living creature has an electric field. Do other mammals suffer arrhythmia in the same way humans do, including pregnancy?

Certain sports people can slow their heartbeat down. Golfers and marksmen are examples. The slowing of the heart increases the accuracy of the shot. It is not done consciously, but in response to the conscious mind's request for 'quiet' whilst focussing on the task in hand. There are two options for fit and healthy people having vagal tone arrhythmia associated with ESP. The first is, with an exceptionally healthy heart there is a greater sensitivity to the electric field pulses. The second is the reverse, if there is an existing sensitivity to electric field pulses then the heart is permanently being exercised beyond normal 'pumping' duties, even at rest. This may be an explanation as to my slimness, despite the large appetite.

Chapter 7: Creatures of the night

How do dreams come into this and what do they mean? Let's start with differences between being awake and asleep. Whilst awake we take in the world through our senses, and consciously relate to surroundings, drawing on experience and senses to guide us. When asleep we still have some awareness of our surroundings. A work colleague told of when a giant crab scuttled down the wall of his bedroom. He woke with a start discovering the picture hung on his wall had fallen behind the bed. This tells us senses are taking in the world while we sleep and dream. Interestingly he would have only heard the picture fall, but in his dream he saw it. A case of experience in one sense interpreted into another.

One of the main differences between sleeping and waking is our physical interaction; the brain sends chemicals stopping signals to the muscles, in effect, paralyzing us. I have often felt like a bystander during dreams. Whilst asleep the sub-conscious mind is in charge and the conscious mind, in effect, knocked out, or standing helpless to one side. My waking thoughts are in English. The darker my dreams are, the more language reduces and raw emotion takes place. The ones containing terror have no words. Even on the nights when my dream thoughts were the same as my waking thoughts, it was despair and anxiety which came across, not words.

Dreams have been a topic of discussion, probably since we began to talk. Ideas have been put forward to the meaning of dreams. There are no universal meanings, they are an individual's interpretation of experiences and memories. Asking what a dream means makes as much sense as asking what waking thoughts mean, or what the shapes and images in clouds are. We all see different things, even when pointed out to others, they do not see the shapes in the same way we do.

Three types of dream are of interest, hag phenomena,

night terrors and an unnamed one. You wake, unable to move. There's an awareness, of someone, something, a shadowy creature in the room, it may be pressing down on your chest. You are paralysed, anxious, terrified. Eventually you wake properly and can move. This is hag phenomena, also called sleep paralysis. Science explains it as the crossover from sleeping to waking. Chemicals in the bloodstream prevent muscles from working, just for a few seconds. There may also be images and a pain in your chest.

A night terror is a feeling of terror during sleep. The hallmark of a night terror is its inconsolable nature. It shows itself as a dream or nightmare.

As a sufferer of hag phenomena and night terrors, they are much the same. Hag phenomena concerns a presence and an inability to move, but otherwise is a night terror. The terror is neither the worst nor the strongest ever experienced, however, it does not leave, remaining in your chest, like a lump in the throat after you've woken. Simply, the experts have completely misunderstood both. They are picking up another person's heartbeat, 'listening' to an emotional and health state. The process of 'listening' increases the heartbeat by about 20%. This in turn switches on anxiety giving rise to the sense of terror. This terror is always going to be extreme since it comes from inside. People who have episodes of hag phenomena or night terrors are likely to have some mental disorders, depression, anxiety, personality disorders, narcolepsy, sleep apnoea to name a few. It makes sense, because the individual is being bombarded on an emotional level by at least one other person. Neither the sufferer nor the person they are picking up from is consciously aware of this communication happening. Sufferers are likely to have panic attacks, as characterised by the following physical symptoms;-

- a sensation your heart is beating irregularly
- sweating

- trembling
- shortness of breath
- a choking sensation
- chest pain
- feeling sick

For the sufferer it ranges from frightening, to feeling like 'someone reading over your shoulder'. Panic attacks happen in people who have hag phenomena because they are the same thing, one awake, and the other asleep. The conscious mind is reading it differently from the subconscious mind that looks after sleep.

The unnamed type of dream is not treated, quite simply because no one complains of it. It is a night terror with a difference. The person who has it is no longer terrified; they accept it, a moment to enjoy. Often exhilarating, like skydiving. The few people I talk to who have experienced this type of dream seem to share common attributes. They are self-aware, intelligent, at ease with themselves and live life their way, not the way others demand. If male they seem to be in touch with their 'feminine' side, and they appear to have strong introvert qualities, and hidden depths. Hardly surprising, having to keep such dreams within yourself, dreams which others find so peculiar. Introverts are usually more aware of their surroundings from birth than others. Many are involved in the art world. Is this because they have been listening to ESP signals since before they were born? I work in the theatre industry so this is hardly conclusive, if only because of not meeting many scientific types in my field to compare with.

In 2012 on the return flight from a yoga retreat, I sat with two ladies from the yoga group. Neither of whom knew anything about my thoughts on ESP. The flight was bumpy, and scaring one of them. I said to her it was like being on a fairground ride, and anyway it didn't compare to the excitement or exhilaration of my falling-flying dream, which I related. She suddenly became thoughtful, "I had a dream once. There was this dark figure in the room with me. It was really scary". I said "And no one believed you about how terrifying it was, and when you woke up it wouldn't go away?" "No they didn't, and it didn't go". I asked if any of her friends or family were having a difficult time then. She replied "No, it was thirty two years ago, I was pregnant".

The falling/flying sensation in dreams is not unusual. The most likely reason is the signal from the balance organ is not being received and therefore it feels like you are weightless. It is possible the brain part which normally deals with balance is listening to the heart instead. This would give the sense of falling/flying at the same time as picking up terror from the heart. Some of my dreams include floating up and down stairs, and streets. This might be being receptive to picking up ESP, but drawing a 'blank'.

Now for a creature of the day; day-dreaming. The greatest amount of day-dreaming was during secondary school, when my parents were splitting up. Everybody complained about it. Hard to understand why, it is an enjoyable escape, which if I'm allowed to wake up from of my own accord leaves me feeling relaxed and refreshed. My explanation for day-dreaming is vagal tone taking command of your mind, exerting and exercising itself. Not only does it co-ordinate your organs, also your feelings and emotions, repairing you. Children with parental problems appear distant and indulge in day-dreaming. Rather than making them 'pay attention', would it not be better to allow mending to happen? Which is more important learning a school lesson, or sorting your head out? My experience of day-dreaming is it should be encouraged rather than frowned upon. It is something we lose the ability to do as adults. Then struggle to get it back, settling for 'meditation' instead.

Chapter 8: Hugging is good for you

Hugging is recognised as good for you. There have been studies into the positive effects. It increases natural 'happy chemicals' oxytocin, serotonin and endorphins; it helps the heart, lowers blood pressure by inducing vagal tone; Reduces cortisol, a stress hormone. What isn't there to love about a genuine proper hug?

The most important part of meeting Jane was the goodbye hug. We stood holding each other relaxed, motionless, for at least 10 seconds. Looking back it seems our hearts learnt to recognise each other's beat. How would hearts remember? There are two options here. The memory is stored in our brain; or, the heart has a way of remembering. It's recently been shown neurons exist in the heart, with talk of them making decisions. Neurons are not merely decision takers, they make decisions based upon experience. Unlike a computer where memory and processors are separate, in people and animals memory is integral to making decisions. It is as though the memories themselves make decisions. If the heart does remember there is at least one precedent for other senses having memory, though not with neurons. The nose holds onto molecules that have been smelled for up to six weeks.

We learn to recognise faces from birth. Each and every person's face is made up of muscles with unique lines, creases and blemishes developed through life. Each heart is unique in the same way, made up of muscles with lines, creases and blemishes. As the heart beats and changes shape this unique signature imposes itself on the generated electric pulse. Like a face it will show emotional characteristics. If the heart beats 'anxiously' this will appear in the pulse the same way as anxiety on a person's face. We recognise a face in the crowd, likewise a heartbeat can be recognised. Like picking out a child's voice in the playground despite the background noise. Every mother has heard her child scream in true pain, it is piercing, cutting through all other sounds. The memory of a person's heartbeat is likely to be used as a filter. Filters and 'sorters' exist in many of our senses. The ear sorts quiet and loud sounds. Eyes filter strong and weak light. A squid is able to detect polarised light. Some filters and sorters are not controlled by the brain. They are naturally occurring parts of the sensory organs. It makes sense the heart is responsible not only for its own filtering, but its own recognition unlike the other senses where the brain is responsible for recognition.

The recognition of heart beats and interaction of electric fields explains why some people enjoy hugging so much; and are good at it. It may point to other happenings between people. Why the loss of someone, especially in couples who have been together for a long time is so devastating; as though they no longer hear the comforting sound of their partners voice. Vagal tone may require occasional external nudging to keep working at optimum, hugging would do this. Empathy is not some psychological mumbo-jumbo, it's a real physical effect of and from the heart.

We seem blind to what happens inside of ourselves. Senses are often confused with each other, substituting one for another. Sex, love and affection are based upon touch; yet we watch porn, and read romantic novels. Indulging in lifestyles to cram our senses with ever greater and stronger feelings. Drugs, sex, food, thrills and excitements; nothing seems to satisfy our appetites. This is an odd contradiction, we do not suffer sensory problems as much as we do emotional, yet we turn to the senses to resolve emotional issues. Teenage anxiety and depression is considered a serious problem for the developed world. It may be the world is putting undue pressure to succeed, and much of their environment is based on being sold something. They are getting messages which are interfering with emotional and ESP based development; causing behaviours which are hurtful and damaging to others around them. We are more civilised now than ever before in history, yet our behaviour is more destructive than all of history's barbaric hordes put together. Indulging in sexual gratification as a replacement for love and affection. It has become worse through our lifestyles where we barely interact let alone touch. Barriers are created and justified by clothing, laws, technology and rights to name a few. I'm not sure about tree huggers, but I'm sure about people hugging. It only works if both enjoy hugging each other, and works best if the hug is motionless with a silent relaxed mind, in the moment. You cannot force someone to like or love you through it. There are those who would use it as an excuse for sexual gratification. These are old observations, but observers have been unable to say why. Now though, we may have a reason science can explore.

What isn't there to love about a genuine proper hug?

Chapter 9: Art and science

Art: *The expression or application of human creative skill and imagination, typically in a visual form such as painting or sculpture, producing works to be appreciated primarily for their beauty or emotional power.*

The key words in the above definition are 'creative', 'imagination' and 'emotional'.

Creative: *Relating to or involving the use of the imagination or original ideas to create something.*

Imagination: *The faculty or action of forming new ideas, or images or concepts of external objects not present to the senses.*

Emotional: *Poignant, moving, touching, affecting, powerful, stirring, emotive, heart-rending, heart-breaking, heart-warming, soul-stirring, uplifting, impassioned, dramatic.*

Creativity is putting imagination to work. Imagination is from within, bypassing the normal senses. Emotional is described as a sense with strong emphasis on the heart, but without using external senses.

So Art, is an idea from the mind of the artist which 'speaks' to the viewer, mainly in the heart.

Music: *Vocal or instrumental sounds (or both) combined in such a way as to produce beauty of form, harmony, and expression of emotion.*

Harmony: *A pleasing combination of elements in a whole.*

Emotion, again. This sounds similar to vagal tone. Research in Sweden has revealed singers in a choir harmonise their voices and heartbeats. They have not offered an explanation. It may be quite simply to sing together, we have to breathe the same, and therefore the hearts tend to beat in time, more likely, there is something further to it. Certainly singing in a choir is good for your heart. Even without ESP involvement, it may be the electric field or pulse generated by a group helps the heartbeat of individuals.

Of the Arts music is the most universal, cutting across cultural, class and age divides. It is capable of evoking a wave of emotional response from the listener, especially when a human voice is added. The lyrics themselves do not necessarily add to the emotion. I am always surprised at the mundane content of many songs, though there are also touching lyrics. Our hearing is particularly sensitive to the range of the human voice. Music calls strongest to teenagers who feel able to swamp themselves in its relief, and escape from the world.

With all these definitions of art and its associations the brain does not get a single mention. Emotion, the state of mind, is what unifies these arts. The brain is involved in getting art out, but in terms of the original formation it is involved as much as it is in hearing a sound.

Literature: *Written works, especially those considered of superior or lasting artistic merit.*

In Shakespeare there is the use of the iambic pentameter. This is where stress is alternated. Say to yourself;-

"Dee-dah, dee-dah, dee-dah, dee-dah, dee-dah, dee-dah, dee-dum"

This is an example of alternating stress. It gives rhythm and flow to the structure. Everyday sentences often have this form since it is comfortable and natural to use. Some people find it easy to do regardless of class or education; you might be one of those people, doing so without realising it. English is fortunate, it absorbs words, takes and creates new grammar all the time. To call it English is a misnomer, it is a melting pot for many languages. Infamously difficult to learn, but a delight to use since it grows with the needs of users, rather than bureaucratic rules. This natural growth has allowed it to take on the iambic pentameter, like a heartbeat. It is not only English which has such forms. Haiku, a Japanese poem should be utter-able in one breathe. Structures and use of language are linked to breath and heartbeats. It is unsurprising since we use our breath to speak, but it is easy to overlook.

The actual words we use speak volumes about meanings. It is almost impossible to talk about emotions or feelings without mentioning the heart or the processes it involves. We fall in love at first sight, the heart pounds in our chest. We are flushed with sexual excitement. Hearts miss a beat. There follows a popular story, originally by the Rev, Garry Izzard;-

A young man once stood on a street corner, opened his coat, and cried, "Look at my heart, look at my perfect, perfect heart." A crowd soon gathered, impressed by his perfect heart. They stood in awe of a heart without blemish, perfect and complete in every way.

Soon an old man walked by and paused to see what the commotion was all about. When he heard the young man proudly crying "Look at my perfect heart" the old man pushed his way to the front to get a closer look. And when he saw the young man's heart he scolded him. "Son, that's not a perfect heart. If you want to see a perfect heart you need to see mine." With that the old man opened his coat to reveal an old, knotted and ugly heart. It was full of bumps and holes, and pieces of it had broken off here and there.

The crowd began to laugh, but the old man raised his hand and began to speak. "See this bump" he said,

"That's when I met my first love. Oh, how the sun shone that day, how bright the colours of the universe were, how sweet the singing of the birds in the trees. What a wonderful moment it was...Ah, but see this hole, that's when my first love and I broke up. How it pained me, and pains me still. But the hole once ran much deeper. The years have managed to fill it in a lot...See this bump, that's when I met the woman who became my life partner. Oh, what a wonderful life we had – year after year of shared companionship, of laughter, tears and joy. This scratch here is when we had a blazing row that threatened to end our marriage – but we made up and moved on...Over here, this place where a piece of my heart has been broken off, this is when she passed away. Oh the ache – yes it still aches even today, for she took a part of my heart to the grave with her, but I trust she will return it to me someday...Ah, but here's another great bump. This was when we began our family. You'll notice the hole beside it. That's when we learned we could not bear our own children. How hard it was to accept, how painful to live with. But the bump is when we got our adopted daughter – our very own beautiful little girl to raise as our own. And yes, there are scratches and indentations surrounding the bump – the times we fought and yelled. But always we learned to forgive, and so this bump grows ever bigger."

The old man went on to describe many other bumps and holes and scratches on his heart, and when he finished the crowd was silent. "You see son" he said, turning to the young man with the unblemished heart, "yours is not a perfect heart, for it has not lived, it has not been touched with joy and tears and laughter and love and pain and anguish and hardship and celebration. Only when you are an old man like me will you be able to look upon a gnarled and battered heart and be able to say, 'yes, now that is a perfect heart.'"

Science: *The intellectual and practical activity encompassing the systematic study of the structure and behaviour of the physical and natural world through observation and experiment.*

In the Art world emotion, creativity, passion, all converge on the heart. Science regards the heart as a remarkable biologically engineered pump. Why the difference of opinion?

Science tries to make sense of the world. It builds a picture of the rules and regulations governing our universe. Continually re-traces its steps to redefine what was previously thought to be true. From the way the universe works, to the number of ribs in a man's body. Every conceivable scientific truth has at some time in the past been a different truth. Scientists experiment and analyse data to come up with an idea of how things work. Don't they?

Chemistry is about interaction of electrons in atoms. Millikan is regarded as the father of modern chemistry. He performed an experiment to discover the charge on an electron. Droplets of oil, charged plates, measurements. Loads of maths. Then lo' and behold he calculated the charge of an electron. There is however, a problem. Results which did not fit his model were ignored. He assumed they were wrong, believing he already knew the charge on an electron and was in effect proving his belief to be correct. Ironically if he had been honest with his results, instead of discarding them, science would have moved forward about fifty years. He is not alone in doing this, facts are often proven to fit the theory. Facts which don't fit are called singularities, anomalies or experimental error, and are usually ignored. It has been useful for science, people driven by their belief have genuinely been able to prove when everyone else thought differently. It has also been the source of much trouble. For hundreds of years the medical world believed a man had twenty three ribs, because the bible said Eve was made from one of

Adam's ribs. Anyone who argued against this would at best have been outcast, at worst accused of heresy and killed.

Belief: *An acceptance that something exists or is true, especially one without proof.*

In school everyone was taught our fingers and toes wrinkled when bathing because of osmosis, where water is absorbed into the skin. Making our skin bigger and therefore wrinkly. It has since been discovered wrinkling is due to the brain telling skin to wrinkle; so, not osmosis. Current theory is it gives better grip for holding wet objects. This may be true, but can only be a small part of its significance. Our toes also wrinkle, underneath and on top. Toes are used for balance, they do not hold onto things, even the ground. Other parts of our bodies show signs of this wrinkling and changing texture. The same wrinkling happens under different circumstances, Raynauds for example. What can be said is the current explanation is poor.

Art is about trying new things, breaking away from rules, creating something which has not previously existed. Science is about discovering rules, defining characteristics of the universe, finding out what makes everything tick.

Religion: *The belief in and worship of a superhuman controlling power, especially a personal God or gods.*

Fraudster: *Someone who gets money by deceiving people.*

Faker: *Imposter, someone who makes deceitful pretences.*

Self-deception: *The action or practice of allowing oneself to believe that a false or unvalidated feeling, idea, or situation is true.*

Science, religion and art will attract particular types of people. Each has their own special appeal, whether it is truth, rules, acceptance, money, influence or power. There are several possible reasons science has not unravelled ESP.

My own extreme experience on the night Jane rang increased my artistic output, though it owed much to the situation at the time. Painting, writing, card making all increased. If this is true for other individuals with ESP experiences, they will move to the world of art. This is most likely to occur during teenage formative years when career choices are being made and vagal tone is at its highest. People involved in science may have no experience of ESP. It is then hard for them to believe in something they have not seen for themselves. We have all been guilty of disbelieving others until presented with hard evidence. The reverse is true, conjurors and tricksters have either convinced us of, or made us experience something false, causing belief in a deception.

Science and especially medicine have become vast monolithic institutions. Players have become remote. They don't talk to each other, seeing only value in their own work. When talking with David he briefly showed his frustration with others in psychology where ego is more important than knowledge.

The laws and rules science uses as building blocks have become so ingrained as to be immutable in the minds of scientists and workers it involves. Many may not understand the laws, but cling to them, a life jacket in a sea storm. When George, the psychologist became so angry, he was like a priest clutching the holy book to his chest and screaming 'heresy'. The fact neither he, nor the GP, in their reports made any mention of what I said casts the medical world in a poor light. How many others being treated have reported happenings or incidents to medical experts and been ignored. Over recent years it has been discovered many high level animal species have homosexual individuals. When talking with naturalists they admitted to having observed this, but did not report so since they presumed it was an anomaly. I personally do not believe in little green men, however, how can we really know if professionals are selective about their reporting?

"All art constantly aspires towards the condition of music"
Walter Pater 1839- 1894

This observation has been made many times. It may well be music parallels the emotional state in a human best of the arts. Music certainly speaks to us, it gives comfort in the loneliness of the rush hour and ecstasy in the group, having the most exposure of any art form. In my darkest time when there was no help, and those I had genuine affection for turned away from me, music was my companion.

I will add a statement about science.

"All science constantly aspires towards the condition of religion"

Chapter 10: Silence is golden

Twins are more likely to have late speech development than single children. There are theories why (including the specialists' who saw Angelica). It is ESP, because if they have it there is a chance to practice with each other in the womb. Knowing the percentage of twins who are late speakers would tell us how many people have this ability across the population. It is probably these same twins who in later life say they know when something is wrong with the other. One aspect which appears to contradict ESP occurring before birth, is arrhythmia in unborn children is relatively rare. It's possible either late speech development or arrhythmia are not related to ESP; or, either an unborn child has such a high vagal tone as to be completely adaptable; or the inert heart chamber is able to accept the pulses without interrupting the rest of the heart.

For my late speech development I was completely unaware of the problem, though do remember using the tape recorder. This worked where all else failed for a simple reason, all previous attempts were with people on a face to face basis. The tape recorder had no heart beat and therefore only sound to be sensed. This implies a confusion between my brain, ears, heart and tongue. The ears listened to sounds, the heart picked up the emotions, but presumably when the language part of my brain triggered it tried to speak with the heart. Whilst the heart beats it is always sending emotions. This is likely the reason once speech started I became a chatterbox, continually talking with my heart, even if no one seemed to listen.

Spoken language is comprised of naturally occurring elements and learnt elements. Emotional tone, stress patterns, a child's scream of physical pain are natural, these all trigger automatic responses within ourselves; responses we are born with. Words, sentence construction and the content of speech, are responses learnt as we grow.

The naturally occurring parts of language must have developed over millions of years. As mammals, by definition, the heart beat and giving birth to live young have been in existence for as long as we have. This means communication from the heart is older than spoken language. Spoken language is more effective as a communication tool than picking up emotions from heart beats. Nature tends not to remove evolved traits when they are no longer useful. Our appendix has no discernible use, it is reduced, yet still exists. When a foetus develops it goes through various stages, some of which stop or change, for a brief moment as foetuses we develop gills. Elements of ESP have made their way into spoken language, and the emotional response still exists. ESP in humans is on its way out in evolutionary terms. So I'm not the future, but a throwback.

Other mammals should show signs of this ability. There are senses in animals yet to be discovered. In zoos newborns are sometimes taken from the parents for medical care and treatment. Keepers have noticed, especial with high level apes like gorillas, if the young have died the mother seems to know, though she could not have seen or heard them. Mammals most likely to have the ESP ability are apes, being social animals able to hug each other. Elephants, having a two year pregnancy. Giraffes, for their powerful heart, and finally marine mammals since oceans contain creatures able to handle electricity. If marine mammals have this, the signal will travel in a different way simply because there is no electrical difference in the water. It is also more likely to travel in a 3-dimensional manner. This will allow them to send emotions to depths, but will probably reduce the distance it can be sent over. Outward signs of ESP are empathy. Mammals tend to have this. Owners of cats and dogs know their pets care for them when they are ill or anxious. There are numerous examples on social media of empathy between different animals. Birds may have ESP and empathy because of their extraordinary breathe control which is needed to sustain flight; breathing and the flapping of the wings are connected. Their singing ability is likely be linked to the heart.

Like many people I talk to myself. Embarrassingly loudly at times. In yoga during breath control we are often told to count for each breath. I find this difficult and awkward, my breath tends to jerk with the counting. The breathing alters in line with my thinking of each number. This change in breathing will reflect in the heartbeat. The best yoga practice is achieved through visualisations. A good teacher will say something like "Imagine you are being pulled and stretched through both hands as you extend outwards". Visualisations avoid thinking in words leading to smoother breathing. With swimmers it is noticeable some are jerky in their movement and swim ineffectively. It may be from using the instructions of words in their head rather than letting go and flowing with the movement.

If ESP control mechanisms are linked to our speech and language centres this explains in part how we are sometimes aware of another person's thoughts. There is no doubt context, other senses and previous experience are involved. When we know what someone else is thinking, it's as though we hear their voice in our head. As they think their thoughts the breath alters whilst silently speaking words. The heart beat changes with the breath, it is this alteration we are picking up. Like lip reading.

People who are multi-lingual often think in the different languages. Thinking is involved with sound and listening, how often have you found it too noisy to think? There appear to be three different waking states to listening and thinking. There is Cacophony, when there is busy noise inside and out. Unfortunately this is the most common state we find ourselves in, sometimes self-inflicted. There is Harmony, listening to music, or enjoying the company of a small group of like-minded people. Finally there is Silence or Stillness, some people are uncomfortable with this. For myself it comes with underwater swimming, daydreaming and occasionally in yoga whilst doing the 'corpse' pose. Several times a worried teacher has woken me from this pose before now. Presumably these three conditions also occur during sleep, except then the subconscious is in charge.

Spoken language reflects much about us. We use words which fit, and sound right. Despite the synthetic nature of language our sub-conscious drives much of it. Terror, horror and fear are often used to mean the same thing; yet what do they actually mean? Terror comes from inside, it is part of our nature and often difficult to put into words. Horror is taught and reflects cultural values. It is a form of disgust, a horror in one culture is seen as normal in another. Tracy Emin's 'My Bed' is an excellent example of this, I feel sure many a teenager's Mother would agree about horror. Fear is learnt from experience. Like discovering certain plants sting or insects bite. A notable difference in the forms of horror and terror are, 'horrific' and 'terrific'. Here they are nothing like each other, terrific is exciting and thrilling, a night terror someone has learnt to accept. I can only vouch for English, other languages will have to speak for themselves.

We think using words, at least we do when awake. This presents an interesting point. Other animals, presumably think using a combination of instinct, experience and immediate sensory information. There is an honesty to the way most animals live, which is missing from human beings. Children still possess it; until we teach them to speak. Is it because we think using words? Words are an amazing form of communication. With them we are able to have specialists, teachers, who can pass knowledge which has taken generations to gather. Storytelling, unsurpassed in nature has evolved, and gives pleasure to young and old alike. Yet we are often unable to tell truth from fiction, placing a reliance on belief and leaders instead.

Several times baby's mothers have said "Oh no, he/she doesn't like anyone else to hold them, just me". In my mid-twenties I discovered a technique for holding babies who do not enjoy being held by strangers. Hold the baby gently, rest their head against your chest, and then hum so your chest vibrates. You only need do this for a few seconds whilst they become comfortable resting against your chest. Then they listen to your heartbeat. It does not work every time, but often is effective.

Chapter 11: Long distance call

Picking up Jane's anxiety from 6,000 miles is extreme, though not necessarily unique. Even the tiniest effect on a force or energy can travel vast distances. In our solar system planets, asteroids and comets orbit the sun. There are fragments of dust, even atoms orbiting the sun from millions of miles away each exerting a small gravitational force. Solar flares cause an answering electrical pulse from the earth, for these forces distance is no object. With regard to ESP on earth there is a large amount of background noise, and 6,000 miles is roughly a quarter of the earth's circumference, so a direct route looks impossible.

There seem only three possibilities for this signal, or pulse, to travel such distance using the electric field. The following descriptions are crude and suffer inaccuracies, but provide adequate models;-

I. Bouncing off the ionosphere, similar to the way long wave radio is transmitted. It would reduce the quality of the signal and be likely to encounter noise. It would also be emitted three-dimensionally (solid, like a cube), up and down, as well as along. This requires more energy than either two-dimensions (flat, like a sheet of paper) or one-dimension (linear, like a thread). It would need to bounce several times to cover the distance.

II. Travelling across the earth's surface. The earth and the atmosphere have different electrical characteristics, this would mean the signal would be sandwiched between the two layers (like a ship travelling on the surface of the water). This would be two-dimensional, but still encounter noise on a crowded plane, and be subject to undulations and rifts in the earth's surface.

III. The electrical difference between the earth and the

atmosphere increases as we rise through the atmosphere. If the signal was to travel at a specific height in the atmosphere's electrical difference, it would be like dropping a pebble into a pool of water. The ripples would spread out following the contour of the earth. This is two-dimensional and would still encounter noise, but much less than the other models. The undulations in the earth's surface are less pronounced as you rise through the electric field.

The first one seems unlikely, it would be more distorted than the other two and require the most energy. Nature tends to be smarter and more efficient than we give it credit for. The second one, if it worked would encounter all other electric waves in this single plane and be subject to noise. The third choice shows the most promise, it deals with the electric field in a way which seems to be an unexplored area of science.

It is presumed the third choice is how Jane's anxiety travelled. Moving up away from the earth there is an increase in the electrical difference of about 120 volts per metre. It eventually peaks at about 300,000 volts. It shows up where there are breaks in this field, a ship's mast will cause sparking called St. Elmo's fire, and lightning strikes are a ferocious example of the electrical difference. If a pulse is sent through an electric field it will have a wavelength, like the height of waves coming into the seashore. It will have a preferred voltage difference (height) to travel at. The human heart will use a specific layer of electrical field to send pulses through relating to its size, shape, etc... The wavelengths will be big for two reasons. First, the amount of energy for a large wavelength is less than for a small wavelength, so a greater distance can be covered by the same energy. Secondly a large wave length is more likely to be received. If it travels at about three metres from the ground, and the wavelength is only a couple of centimetres the recipient might not be in the right place to sense it. If the wavelength is 100 metres long then, unless they were deep underground or in an airplane, it would be felt.

Other mammals and creatures have different size and shape hearts following different beats. This means they may use ESP in different layers of the electric field. There is far less noise in this form of communication than the other possibilities. People in the telecoms industry might see possibilities for a new type of mobile signal which reduces the number of masts. The potential for such technology is great; hospital patients could be monitored without wires, care homes could know the welfare of its occupants without intrusion. It might even be usable as a terrorist detector, picking up the anxiety of someone about to commit an outrage.

People often hold their breath during a normal day: In a situation they do not wish to interrupt, whilst listening to a close and personal conversation, or in a fight or flight situation. Both nights Jane rang were characterised by the violent gasping breath upon waking. It would make sense it's related to the distance since it only happened on those two nights. Using a panic attack as the model, my heartbeat would have risen by about $20 - 25\%$. The pulse in the electric field would have been weak and difficult to make out. It is likely the breath was held whilst listening to her anxiety. Like straining your ears and holding your breathe to hear a faint voice far away. It must have been held for more than a few seconds. Considering the effect, I feel it must have been at the limits. If she had been further away, would it have been picked up at all, or would my reaction have been more violent?

Chapter 12: The deep end

This chapter is about taking thoughts further and involves wild speculation. The subject matter is already contentious, so now is not the time to be a shrinking violet, it is the time to dive into the deep end.

The way a mother communicates with her unborn child using chemicals, hormones and electric pulses has consequences for cloning. Plans to use other animals to incubate lost species, such as Woolly Mammoths, Tasmanian Devils, etc... may need to be reconsidered. Part of what we call our humanity might be learned through electric pulses. Anxiety is known to be transmitted to unborn children, why not other characteristics.

It is hard to know which aspects of ESP are inherited, and which nurtured. Kind-hearted by nature has been mentioned; this may be false, it might be learnt. I dealt with people from an early age who showed antagonistic tendencies, in Madge's case ESP was not needed to detect this. It is almost certain their heartbeats contained negative emotions. This would have been distressing. I probably discovered being kind and nice to people gave them a 'happy' heartbeat; or at least leaving them so as not to feel their negative emotions. It would have been good for myself, like harmony in a choir. It would have encouraged me to help people regularly, which I do.

Even though Angelica and Glenda learnt to speak late; it may have been partly genetic in Angelica's case because of the acute awareness from birth; it was certainly partly learned by both of them being carried against my chest in a sling.

It's likely there is no choice in having ESP communication with members of your family, however, with others there may be some choice. I have never locked eyes with a man, therefore presumably choose this situation on the basis of sexual preference. In Jane's case it could be said there was limited choice, the other senses pulled me to her. When it came to hugging, again initially it appears there was choice. However, Jane is an open hearted, vivacious and tactile person, so maybe not as much choice as you'd think; plus we both liked each other.

Angels and demons, representatives of good and bad are constant in history and culture, even today; ESP is a foundation of their existence. Demons are obvious in hag phenomena. The name itself comes from the knowledge people awoke to discover a demon, or hag, in the room with them, sometimes sitting on their chest, making it hard to breathe. One of mine, was the Minotaur-like creature chasing me in dark dreams as a child. Graham and I agree the reason for it being a Minotaur is we enjoyed Greek myths as soon as we could read. My mind interpreted the ESP visually and it fitted the interpretation, and its characteristics matched Graham. This brings reality into dreams, apparently we do not dream of strangers. Science could consider bringing hag phenomena and not dreaming of strangers together. According to scientific understanding the hag has to be based upon someone or something. So like Frankenstein's monster our nightmare demons are composed from bits of reality. If those dreams are ESP inspired, the terror is real.

Angels though less obvious, are culturally as common as demons. People who seem to appear when needed are definitely angels. There are people who arrive at just the right time. I have this ability with specific individuals. It is so pronounced I walk into their office whilst talking with them on the phone, or they look up from their desk to say "I was just about to call you". When it happens several times they inevitably ask "How do you do that?" It is certainly true that people who do this are regarded as angels in terms of the help they give. Angels and demons are important figures in the art world, often representing extremes of the mind; fear, love, terror.

Angels occur in modern culture. Comic books are filled with such characters, individuals tortured by pain and anxiety. Often they wear capes rather than wings, odd when you realise in day to day life no one wears a cape. Having said that, it's also odd they wear their underpants on the outside. These characters evoke something in ourselves which we relate to, even if we cannot put it into words. The most compelling stories are not about their powers, but sufferings and sacrifices. On a human level, do only selfless angels dream of demanding demons? In other words, people who are sensitive to ESP and have night terrors or hag phenomena are angels within our society.

Human ESP ability is certainly in decline. Speech is superior to ESP as a form of communication in most respects. More than 90% of the population start to speak by 2 years of age. It is highly adaptive, each culture has a language to deal with its own issues. English is able to absorb words and phrases from other languages, making it reflect current trends. Using language it is possible to have a communication with someone you have never met before. We've had speech long enough to have developed a genetic pre-disposition to it, some of which has crossed over from ESP. Speech will almost inevitably win when it competes with ESP for brain power. Modern society is keen on education and a prescriptive approach to learning. There is pressure to learn more, faster and earlier. Language is only one component of this. Despite all we are told, questioning 'Truth' is seen as wasteful, counter-productive and symptomatic of ignorance. We are exposed to words now more than ever before. Much of this is through modern media which contains no heartbeat. Language has drawbacks. Lying and storytelling are a standard part of life. Speech allows miscommunication, whether intentional or not.

The earth's magnetic field is in transition and becoming weaker. The electric and magnetic fields are related. It is not noticeable in a single lifetime, but over hundreds of generations it is weakening substantially. This weakening of the field will reduce the distance and strength of the pulses.

The impact of modern society is not to be underestimated. There is a determination in the world to have equality of opportunity across all bands of society. The major tool in doing so is education. All children in the developed world are going to school, something previous generations could only dream of. The rest of the world is attempting, and may well succeed in the next few decades to emulate this. Reading, writing and arithmetic are the foundations. The ability to talk is expected as a matter of course. From birth we are exposed to modern media which in almost every case includes the spoken word. It is no chance my own talking started by exposure to a tape recorder. Unlike a human, no heartbeat to feel, it was a clear and simple form of communication. Even without the ESP, there was no body language to decipher with the sounds. The push for education is to allow people a greater choice in their future. With a firm educational background there is a wider range of career choice. This is driven by societies and individuals desire to better themselves. There are weaknesses in the system. The pressure to produce results leads to parrot fashion learning, where questioning is apparently encouraged, but only so long as it sticks with the model. Querying the validity of the model itself is usually dealt with crudely. A recent example is fossilised bones. Fossils are originally organic material which has become petrified, the original substance having broken down and no longer existing. It is now realised the originally organic material does still exists within this structure. There have undoubtedly been times in the past when a student queried this disappearance of organic material, to only be repelled with what now looks like patronising and ill-informed replies. Beginners in a subject are encouraged to defer to older and wiser minds when dealing with something new and unknown. The first psychologist who saw me was honest about her ignorance, passing over to her more experienced colleague. He also didn't know, however, responded by hiding his ignorance and resorting to intimidation.

Prior to modern society part of our development was as the dominant tool user; the opposable thumb and our hands are unsurpassed in nature for flexibility. This in turn encouraged speech development. New born babies talk with their faces and hands long before developing speech. The sucking of their hands and fingers is how they start to use their mouths for intricate movement. Some of us continue a version of this into adult life, do you still bite your fingernails? The part of our brains responsible for controlling the hands also controls tongue movement. Many of us use our hands whilst talking, they tend to move to our face when we lie. One famous newsreader gripped the edge of her desk when reading news to prevent talking with her hands. Whilst threading a needle, as the thread passes through the eye a person's tongue may poke from the side of their mouth. Using our hands has loosened our tongues, allowing for speech development.

Ninjutsu and yoga both use hand and finger positioning with breathing as methods to improve self-awareness and control. Each hand posture has different effects. Ninjutsu has many variations on it, one for awareness, and another for intuition, etc... Amongst the talents a ninja is alleged to have is avoiding an attack they are unaware of. This is a trained awareness. Intuition of this kind is always about people. Someone might say "I feel my brother is in trouble", but I have never heard anyone say "I feel my pet cat is in peril." You may feel this is nonsense, that hands and feet have nothing to do with emotions and state of mind. We wring our hands with anxiety; we get cold feet over fearful situations; cold hands, warm heart (Raynauds?). Most of us have experience of these, they are a direct effect of emotions on our extremities.

During my yoga practice sweat forms to the point it will drip and run creating pools of liquid on the mat. In some poses a hand is extended. The pose is held, I look to the palm of my hand. At times the finger tips are wrinkled. This is similar to Raynauds, having wet hands in the bath, and anxiety with sweaty hands. The connection is most likely anxiety chemicals such as adrenaline or cortisol shrinking the blood vessels causing coldness in the extremities. The foods I crave, like ginger, tonic water with quinine, chocolate, substances my body needs, these seem to be chemicals that open blood vessels and allow circulation. These foods all counter the effects of anxiety drugs which my body suddenly produces. It is not a good thing my fingers go cold and would prefer it didn't happen. This implies there is a conflict happening inside of myself. Logic and emotion always seem in conflict. Does my heart have its own mind? It has neurons, brain stuff. A bumble bee has about 80 neurons and we know what a bee can accomplish. If the neurons in the heart are responsible for much of the emotional animal we call a human, and my heart and thoughts struggle with each other; is the heart where the soul resides?

An individual's heartbeat carries a signature of attitude, mood and personality. On its own it will mean little to a community, yet the total of heartbeats may represent the attitude, mood and personality of a community. Something referred to as a hive, or group mind. We are not talking about a conscious entity, nor god. The group heartbeat will have an effect upon individuals including newcomers. They may embrace, or reject this group personality, either way, with other senses, they will detect this community attitude. If you feel this is far-fetched, then please recall the choirs where heartbeats harmonise. Many communities unite behind songs, not just religious ones, think of football. On occasion I have died in dreams, it is distressing. One dream, someone came up behind me, I knew they would shoot me in the back of the head. They shot, it went blank, felt life draining from me. Found I could still think, kept repeating "Make the world better. Make the world better." Is my sub-conscious saying our thoughts and feelings inside make a difference, that we can change the world with positive feelings?

One frustration is almost nothing in this book is new. The arts have at one time or another said these things. In recent times it feels as though their message has been stronger, more frantic, yet the world of science stays remarkably aloof, as though believing it is the only truth. Art believes in equality, science believes inequality. Harsh, maybe. Yet does everything you were taught at school still apply? Can you recall how confidently facts were given? Those teachers and leaders were put in a position of representing past teachings, rather than admit to ignorance or doubt they resorted to a variety of tactics. We have all attended meetings where many people have not understood what is being discussed. This has not stopped anyone, myself included, on speaking to either prove our worth, be part of the team or to show strength of belief. It takes a strong individual to admit ignorance, especially when they are expected to know. When placed in a position of authority it is tempting and easy to fall into the role of fraudster, faker or self-deceiver. The pressure to perform and be guided by career is intense.

Over the last few years I have spoken to people about the subjects this book touches. A well-known sceptic writer for 'Scientific America' said he would devise a test, I still wait. When hearing the explanation for panic attacks one young woman burst into tears. A doctor whose eyes flickered interest upon hearing people with ESP move away from science and towards the arts. It is surprising to learn so few people have locked eyes with anyone else. One man is concerned because he feels he does not love anyone, and never has. The off-duty anaesthetist, who listened patiently thinks it might be true. People who don't agree with my findings have had some professional knowledge and come up with peculiar thoughts of their own that tend to either dismiss the facts, or ignore them. There seem to be many people who don't have these inner emotions. Our success as an animal has been through co-operation. Will our downfall be through conflicts from greed and justifications?

Summary

Most dreams told so far are to do with ESP contact. There have been others, it is hard to know how they fit. One last dream will be related, it is neither hag phenomena nor night terror, but relevant;-

I am a small child, about two years old, in a playground, playing with other children. Suddenly we are attacked by monsters. They are big, green, slime blob monsters. Aggressively they hunt us down, I hide, and watch while they smother and devour screaming running children. It's frightening, but there is nothing to be done. A green slimy blanket is found and cover myself with it. It's possible to move about, but daren't speak because the monsters will realise I'm human and attack. Living like this, no other humans, no friends, no one to talk to. Always moving to stay alive and avoid the monsters; surviving and growing to adulthood. The monsters are trying to be human. They don't talk properly, cannot use tools, have no real hands and are not suited to the world. The decision is made to help them, there is nothing else for me. At one point showing them how to use knives and forks. They notice I'm good at using them. Nodding and saying nothing, knowing if they hear my voice they will realise I'm human and attack me. Desperately wanting to talk, but know doing so is to have them try to change me into one of them. I woke.

My sub-conscious is saying don't let people know about ESP. The price to pay will be derision, anger and fear. The dream also says solitude has to be accepted. There will be those who shall claim to have known all along. Probably courses will be advertised on the internet for exorbitant fees telling you how to stay in emotional touch with loved ones, or how others can be forced into falling in love with you. When the universities join the research it will be called Cardio-Sensory Perception (CSP), followed by in-fighting whilst the relevant departments attempt to exert control over the new subject.

The late speech development, my apparent and infuriating calmness, Night terrors, Raynauds, varicose veins, extreme physical responses to emotion, sweating, panic attacks, the predictive ability for attacks, night cramps, exceptional breathe control, hag phenomena, kind nature, locking eyes. Together they point to a communication at an emotional level between human beings beyond the normal senses. I am a combination of all these, and my own personality of wanting to know why rather than indulge in wishful thinking. Regarding the bizarre nervous breakdown triggered by Jane's phone call. Before then, if asked would my reaction be so extreme, the reply would have been "No". It owed much to the situation as well as ESP, I don't know what the proportions are, but neither can claim all credit. This represents a rare and freak chance to uncover ESP for real. It might be a Pandora's Box, once opened we cannot replace the lid to this knowledge. I seem to be super-sensitive. Jane is no less amazing for sending it over 6,000 miles.

What happens physically and physiologically is debatable, though the heart is the strongest candidate. It is clear the heart and the circulatory system are involved in emotions. We blush, freeze from fear, and go pale with shock. It is almost impossible to think of an emotion which does not affect the heart. If scientists and industrialists are thinking of utilising this form of communication, please, do the research on animals and people before inventing your devices. Mankind has a tendency to invent and 'Hang the consequences'. I would not like to think either a small proportion of people or an entire species being wiped out so we can have cheap phone calls or obscene weapons in the quest for profit, power and glory. Some of my understanding will be wrong. It would be remarkable if everything in this book is correct, but the main thrusts seem difficult to argue against.

Discovering yoga has been a wonderful joy, hard to know whether it is helping or worsening my condition.

Either increasing sensitivity and susceptibility, or strengthening the heart. One reason for saying this is changes in my hands are crazier than ever before. They can be a patchwork of red, blue and purple, cramps in fingers and palms. When travelling on the underground they are often bright, glowing red. I find the underground awkward. In the words of one song *"They're sharing a drink called 'loneliness'".*

The world of science, in particular medicine, is a tower of babel with different sections unable and unwilling to communicate with each other. It feels like fakers, self-deceivers and fraudsters are the key holders to this tower. A place where only bureaucracy rules with no room for imagination or intelligence. The sheer stubborn, self-imposed ignorance of 'professionals' was disheartening. Medicine and science could examine themselves, to look at how blindness has become so wide spread and embedded. It is as though science is so bound with rules and rigidity it has lost vagal tone.

For people who don't have ESP it's hard to convey how wonderful and terrible it is; the loneliness down here, automatic awareness and sense of being different, amazing thrills and terrors in other worlds at night, yet showing a calm dry face to the world. Wishing Jane was still my friend. When she was gone, missed her terribly. I miss her hug. Even though there is no more staring at track from platforms, the memory remains of a phone call at 4:26 a.m.

Acknowledgements:

The majority of information regarding arrhythmia is from "Bennett's Cardiac Arrhythmias. Practical notes on interpretation and treatment, 8th edition" by David H. Bennett.

All dictionary definitions in chapter 9 and the definition of a panic attack are from Wikipedia.

"*All art constantly aspires towards the condition of music*" Walter Pater 1839- 1894.

"The Perfect Heart" is attributed to the Reverend Garry Izzard.

The song referred to in chapter 12 is "Piano man" by Billy Joel.

The research on synchronised heartbeats in choirs was conducted by Sahlgrenska Academy at the University of Gothenburg Sweden, their finding were published by Frontiers in Neuroscience.

Millikan's experiment and it's selectivity over results was questioned by Gerald Holton, a science historian. The errors in it are almost as widely discussed as the experiment itself.

The unreported homosexuality in animals is based on "13 Things that don't make sense" by Michael Brooks.

Helen Middleton
Graham Clark
Kim Mercado
Margaret Adesanya
Norma Castrojeres
Lisa Cleaver
Federica Leonardis
Raphael Casela
Everardo Miranda
St. Mary's school Banbury
Nuffield Health, Ilford

Thank you to the countless people I bored, or freaked out with my endless talking on this subject, your thoughts, opinions and reactions helped shape this book.

CPSIA information can be obtained at www.ICGtesting.com
Printed in the USA
LVOW11s1303070915

453134LV00004B/264/P